"*The Finishing School* is a must-read. It's not just ▮ ▮ 's a meaningful conversation with a frie▮ ▮ nts to give you the very best pract▮ ny important aspects of life. I ca▮ n! Val's writing is sincere, candid,▮ h me over coffee the whole time,▮ ▮ finance to friendship, *The Finishing School* i▮ ▮ked with wisdom from the Word, practical advice, actionable steps, and a whole lot of humor along the way. I'm grabbing a copy (or four) for my own kids to read one day, and for my dearest friends. I can't recommend this unique book enough!"

LARA CASEY,
Author of Make It Happen: Surrender Your Fear, Take the Leap, Live on Purpose. LaraCasey.com.

"In a culture where constant connection and chaotic schedules is praised, *The Finishing School* brings women back to the core of what life is about—faithfully walking with God and chasing after His dreams. Val's simplicity and passion will ignite a passion in your heart to be content with less, live to the fullest, and enjoy the freedom God has given us. Each chapter intentionally walks you through practical steps to living a life of purpose and joy in the midst of our busy days. Val's vulnerability from her own life experiences and wisdom bubbles over from her writing into the reader's life. One thing is sure, God is not finished with us yet, and He will use *The Finishing School* to encourage you to make the most of your days!"

GRETCHEN SAFFLES,
Creator of Life Lived Beautifully, Author of A God-Sized Love Story.
www.lifelivedbeautifully.com

"A few page turns into *The Finishing School* and I knew I'd found a kindred spirit in Valerie Woerner. Valerie's passion for the refinement of our souls gently coaches us along as she provides a framework to think, process and pray through areas of our lives that could benefit from some finishing. I know you'll be appropriately challenged while graciously given space for God's refining work in your life."

JENNI CATRON,
Church leader and author of CLOUT: Discover and Unleash Your God-Given Influence

"If you've ever been overwhelmed by the sheer pressure of life, and struggled with figuring out how to do things 'right', or in a way that ensures God received the glory, *The Finishing School* is your resource. I'll be coming back to this book again and again for guidance when life starts to feel off-balance or out of whack!"

WHITNEY ENGLISH,
Small business consultant and found of Day Designer ®

"I love how Val covers so many topics that we as Christians would like to grow in. It's opened my eyes to areas in my life that I wasn't even aware of that needed more effort and, in other areas, it built confidence to continue. Although so many topics are presented, it is a perfect balance of depth without being overwhelming. The practical tips and extra tools make it simple to remember and implement. It's grown in me a beautiful picture of what a life well learned can look like and gotten me excited to put everything into practice."

NATALIE METREJEAN,
Creator of the Wholeheartedly devotional. NatalieMetrejean.com

"Reading *The Finishing School* felt as though I was sitting in Val's screened-in porch and we were having a cup of coffee just sharing our hearts: feeling both challenged and encouraged by the word of God and a trusted friend. The truth is, this book is timeless and for that it will forever stay on my bookshelf as a resource for life."

MAE SNODGRASS,
Wife, private tutor, woman aiming to soak in God's daily grace

"One of my favorite things about Valerie and the products she makes is that NOTHING is theoretical. *The Finishing School* is no exception. It doesn't just give you ideas, it puts flesh and wisdom on real questions and the workbook provides real steps to take action on what you've learned. What an amazing and valuable tool for the women of our generation!"

JESS CONNOLLY,
Owner of Naptime Diaries Shop, cofounder of The Influence Network, coauthor of upcoming book Wild and Free

"With the world demanding our time and schedules more than ever — the true reward is when we surrender our control to let Him filter through our hearts, habits, and schedules. That is where we find joy. *The Finishing School* shows us what that looks like and how to apply it in our own lives. We fill our calendars and perpetrate the glorification of being busy — perhaps the most important lesson of all is we become better women, servants and children of God when we take time to rest and surrender ourselves in Him."

STEPHANIE STERJOVSKI,
Creative Director: SS Print Shop, Content Creator: SS Life & Style Blog

"*The Finishing School* is a beautiful balance of God's truth and transparency. Val's words do not just inspire, but offer a genuine guide to fill in life's gaps with more of God's best so He gets the glory. Grab a cup of coffee and a highlighter. You're about to make a new friend."

MICHELLE MYERS,

Business mentor and founder of She Works His Way and Cross Training Couture

"*The Finishing School* could not have come at a better time. Valerie has a gentle, affirming yet challenging way to move you from someday to today. You do not feel judged, you just feel like your girlfriend is saying 'I totally get it. I've been there....in fact, I AM there and I know God wants more for us, so let's do this together.' I see a fresh wave of accountability and spurring one another on in the spiritual and life disciplines the Lord is calling us to."

JENN SPRINKLE,

Designer and creative strategist, co-author of 31 days of Prayer for the Dreamer and the Doer, Co-founder of The Well Studio. thewellstudio.co.

"*The Finishing School* was refreshing to my heart, challenging to my pursuit of godliness, and encouraging to my soul. It is a valuable resource at every stage of spiritual life and with Val's easy-to-read writing style it is one that is definitely hard to put down!"

ASHLEY DELAUNE,

Wife, local entrepreneur, girl after a holy heart

"*The Finishing School* is overflowing with practical tips and nuggets of goodness. Valerie's easy, conversational style of writing, combined with her wise, gentle nudges, do one thing: point you to Christ. She's the one-in-a-million big sister you never knew you were missing."

LORIEN OWENS,
Wife and mother of 3, avid reader and adventurer, former delivery girl

"*The Finishing School* is refining and refreshing! Val graciously welcomes readers into her life and home. As she shares practical truths, we are given the opportunity to take part and reflect on areas in our own lives that need a little work and a lot of Jesus! *The Finishing School* invites us not just to read and take in new knowledge, but actively live out the what we've learned."

KATE POWELL,
Photographer & owner of kate&co.

the FINISHING SCHOOL

how one book nerd began living what she learned

VALERIE WOERNER

CONTENTS

To my daughter, Vivi Mae.
I can't wait to see the fair lady you become.

Open Your Books to Page...

A GUIDE TO ORIENTATION

Finishing schools of yesteryear taught about things like posture and etiquette. I'm not here to teach you about that. If I were, I can only imagine the massive book-burning riots that it would ignite. I sit cross-legged on chairs at restaurants. I slouch. I make inappropriate comments at inappropriate times, not on purpose, of course. All the Audrey Hepburn movies in the world haven't changed me, because real change is hard. I may not be passionate enough to change my social graces, or lack thereof, but I am so passionate about the refinement of our soul.

I think we all desire a refined life—the life that testifies to a God who is daily at work in you and me. We want to see fruit that comes from hard work, hardships, and a heart that is being changed by God. We want to taste the victories of seeing God smooth out our rough spots. We will never find perfection this side of heaven, but that doesn't mean God isn't continually shaping us in our pursuit for holiness.

Perhaps my nerdiest quality is my thirst for knowledge. If you tried to strap a book sack to my back and hand me a Scantron and No. 2 pencil, I'd go kicking and screaming. BUT I do get all googly-eyed when I see a new book I want to read and call journaling my thoughts as I learn new things the perfect Friday night. Remember the wise words you learned from Francis Bacon in your school days? Anyone? Anyone? Bueller? Of course you don't, so I'll tell you.

He said "knowledge is power." I couldn't agree more. But one thing I've learned after years of self-help books, business webinars, and conferences is, I *knew* what to do. I just wasn't doing it.

The truth is, we can't stay students forever. We have to put those lessons to the test and embrace the life that awaits us. That's why I like the idea of finishing school. You didn't learn manners for kicks and giggles or to simply be smarter. You learned it to use as you entered society. Finishing school served no purpose if those fair ladies decided to hunker down and make homeroom their forever home. But if you have ever felt like I have, that space of learning is safe. Keeping my nose in a book is terribly comfortable and doesn't really require anything but to consume. The problem is, it's boring and fruitless if we never take the opportunity to exercise what we have learned. James 1:22 says,

> Do not merely listen to the word, and so deceive your-selves. Do what it says. Anyone who listens to the word but does not do what it says is like someone who looks at his face in a mirror and, after looking at himself, goes away and immediately forgets what he looks like. But whoever looks intently into the perfect law that gives freedom, and continues in it—not forgetting what they have heard, but doing it—they will be blessed in what they do.

When we step out with the decided notion that we are being transformed and going to play an active, but submissive role in God's plan, we're blessed. And we blossom. We blossom like an awkward preteen turning into a beautiful, refined young woman.

So where are you today? Do you want to live an intentional life? Do you want to experience all the fruit that God has for you here on earth? I know I do. It's not to pay the down payment on our mansion in heaven. Obedience to God and making an effort to live life more intentionally is not about earning salvation. It's a gift. And that gift should spur us on to live a life that glorifies God.

Our lives should be radically different because of Christ who lives in us. Too often they don't look different. And that's not God's fault. It's our laziness. If we say we are changed but look exactly the same as we always have, why would anyone bother with this whole God thing? The radical transformation that will happen when we get to heaven is exciting to me, but what's also exciting to me is that even in an imperfect world, God is working in me every day to look more like Him right here on earth. We are so privileged that God is a god who not only cares about our eternity but about our life here on earth too.

I am so fired up by this truth. Apart from God, we are a gigantic mess. And with God, we're still a gigantic mess, but one that is loved and being refined because of Christ who lives in us. Christ makes us something new. Any change we make is a direct response from the Lord's work in our lives, and part of His work is putting our very being in motion. God has called us to be His hands and feet. If God wanted to drop food on a homeless man's stoop, He most certainly could. If He wanted you to forgive someone, He could slip a little forgive and forget pill in your water and be done with it. But He instead decides to use us and allow us to be a part of His plan. He desires followers who desire Him, not robots who mindlessly make His plan happen. And lucky for us kids who can't seem to get our hands out of the cookie jar, part of His plan is to grow you and me. To transform us from the inside out and take us from a rebellious toddler to reflections of Him.

We are about to spend a whole book talking about transformation in our lives and how to make progress and become refined by the Lord in our daily lives. My good girl heart has to check my motives when I start getting enthusiastic about DOING. It's all well and good until I leave God out of it. Then it's not so well and good. Writing this book, I had to ask, Am I encouraging others to keep spinning their wheels and focusing on the checklists of a good Christian life?

I really wrestled with this. I didn't want to share a tool that would actually distract from God. Even good things like learning habits or creating some structure can do that. This led me to my Bible to find out how God reconciled faith and works.

A passage that I have clung to for years came to mind: John 15:1-11.

> I am the true vine, and my Father is the gardener. He cuts off every branch in me that bears no fruit, while every branch that does bear fruit he prunes so that it will be even more fruitful. You are already clean because of the word I have spoken to you. Remain in me, as I also remain in you. No branch can bear fruit by itself; it must remain in the vine. Neither can you bear fruit unless you remain in me. I am the vine; you are the branches. If you remain in me and I in you, you will bear much fruit; apart from me you can do nothing. If you do not remain in me, you are like a branch that is thrown away and withers; such branches are picked up, thrown into the fire and burned. If you remain in me and my words remain in you, ask whatever you wish, and it will be done for you. This is to my Father's glory, that you bear much fruit, showing yourselves to be my disciples. As the Father has loved me, so have I loved you. Now remain in my love. If you keep my commands, you will remain in my love, just as I have

kept my Father's commands and remain in his love. I have told you this so that my joy may be in you and that your joy may be complete.

The fruit excites me. The fruit reminds me that God is working in me. It is a testament to His faithfulness and daily presence in my life. The fruit is an outflow of a deep, abiding relationship with the Lord. And my hope is that each chapter will be part of the pruning process that God uses in your life so that you may bear more fruit. Do not leave Him out of this process. That is the key to making sure this doesn't turn into more spinning your wheels.

Fellow Christians, this book is not just about you or me. Our world is hurting, and it's hating Christians because of the behavior they see from so many of us. It's hypocritical, it lacks love, and it's double-minded. When we say one thing and our lives don't reflect that, we aren't serving God's kingdom well. My hope is that you will be encouraged in these pages to live out your faith and that people would see your fruit. This doesn't mean seeking after perfection. It simply means that we look different than we did last year because of God's work in our lives. I think when unbelievers can see our walk—trips and falls and all—that speaks to them too. Let's be genuine and authentic as we pursue Christ and point to His glory.

This book is one part touchy-feely and personal and two parts practical, which is pretty much just like me. Each chapter will have stories from my journey of refinement and what God taught me along the way, as well as practical tips to apply to your own life. There will be a resource page at the end of each chapter with additional resources for further study and links to the worksheets that will help you work through what we talk about. You can print it out at valmariepaper.com/homework (password: fairlady) or if you don't feel like printing, check out our shop (shop.valmariepaper.com) for our Lessons from *The Finishing School* Workbook. I would also recommend keeping a Bible handy and dig into it as the Spirit leads you. You can work through each topic however you like, but here are two suggestions:

1. You can read this book over a year and take steps in each area. There are twenty-four chapters, which works out to reading a chapter, processing the information and working through the homework for one week, and then applying the information and practicing it in your everyday life the following week. This plan allows for six weeks of a break through the year.

2. You can read through the book entirely and ask the Lord to reveal any areas in particular that He wants to park on for a little while longer. Some chapters may be no-brainers for you, while others may step on your toes a bit.

Whatever way makes most sense to you, go for it. I don't want this to be a book that sits on your shelf collecting dust or is read at a surface level. I will be working through this book right along with you. My soul yearns for moments of victory that show the fruit, and my soul even longs for those moments of failure that test and refine me. Fair lady, here's your chance to make a change. I'm rooting you on and am hosting a pep rally in your honor.

Father, I pray for this person reading these words right now, that your truth would shine through on these pages. That my words would fall into the background of the bigger story and plan that you have for them as they read this book. Bless their open heart, as they have chosen to pick this book up to learn more about you and your plan for their life here on earth. In Jesus's name, amen!

Can I just say a quick thank you before we dive in? I am so grateful for the opportunity to share my story with you and pray this will be a life-changing adventure! Feel free to drop me an email at val@valmariepaper.com to share any cool God story that comes as a result of these pages. I would love to celebrate with you!

With so much love and gratefulness,
Valerie

2

Worrier to Warrior

A GUIDE TO PRAYER

If you grew up a worried child like I did, you learned very quickly to drop to your knees and start praying. I was scared of everything. The day we had the fire department come to our school to teach us fire safety, I came home and refused to go inside because a fire might happen. I don't know how long I thought this would last. I was also afraid of the dark and burglars, so when twilight hit, I'd have a big decision to make.

Luckily, my mom, the anti-worrier and the prayer warrior, covered my adolescence in truth and prayer. Before I headed out to camp with our church in the mountains, my mom made sure to send me with encouragement for my ears. I had already had both of my eardrums burst in the past from altitude and pressure, so needless to say, even driving in the mountains made me a basket case. I didn't want to miss out on a good time with my besties, though, so I asked my mom to help me. She printed out a prayer and some verses that I started looking over as soon as I got it in my hands. I made sure it was safely tucked in my Bible before we left. It brought me so much comfort to be in the presence of the Lord and to hear His truth. I needed the reassurance that He was with me, and that prayer did it for me.

A few years later in high school, we started every homeroom with prayer. The person who got to pray also got to write all the prayer requests on the chalkboard. (And if you are going to have to sit in homeroom, you might as well get to write on the chalkboard!) I became the annoying girl who raised her hand every day. *Pick me! Pick me!* Pretty soon no one even volunteered. I had commandeered prayer time without even noticing it.

Most people would rather do a speech than pray in front of people. If you want to see me covered in hives, put me up in front of a room full of people to talk. But ask me to pray in front of that same group, and I'm as cool as a cucumber. I much prefer to know everyone's eyes are closed, heads are bowed, and not a soul is staring at the red patches that might be forming on my neck.

Even at my daughter Vivi's baby shower, the hostesses shared five qualities that my husband, Tyler, hoped Vivi would get from me and one was my quickness to pray. He teased that I would pray for EVERYTHING. To be honest, I had no idea how different this was. I assumed everyone did it, but his view of this as a unique quality reminded me that prayer is a learned skill, and I had spent my young, terrified adolescent and teenage life taking the practice test.

———

Starting this book with the prayer chapter wasn't an accident, and it wasn't just because that's what my business is. It's because prayer can be and should be a part of every chapter that follows. Tim Keller is backing me up on this thought. He shared some incredible words on prayer in his appropriately named book called *Prayer* that helped me realize this was true for everyone and not just the prayer journal girl:

"Prayer is the only entryway into genuine self-knowledge. It is also the main way we experience deep change—the reordering of our loves.... It is the way we know God, the way we finally treat God as God. Prayer is simply the key to everything we need to do and be in life."

So here we are, starting on our journey to a fruit-filled life. I really want this chapter and the next chapter on studying the Bible to lay a solid foundation, because if we don't, the rest is futile. That sounds dramatic, but it's true. Remember John 15:5 that I shared in the last chapter? "I am the vine; you are the branches. If you remain in me and I in you, you will bear much fruit; apart from me you can do nothing."

Maybe you already know that to be true. The million-dollar question is: does your life reflect that? I know it's certainly not always the case for me. That's what this whole book is about—the fruit of what we say we believe. I know I want what I say and what I do to line up. It doesn't mean I'll be perfect, but I hope it means God will be glorified and people will be pointed to Christ when they see me.

Although it is clear prayer is important, I think most of us would say we don't spend adequate time in the presence of the Lord. What is the current state of your prayer life? What things hold you back from deeper communion with Him? One late night while I was writing, I asked y'all on Instagram what stops you from praying or reading your Bible, and you responded:

- you felt it was easy to choose Netflix over prayer time
- you were embarrassed to not have the right words
- you felt you had messed up so much, your prayers didn't deserve to be heard
- you felt like it's just a checklist or talking to the air
- you always got distracted mid-prayer
- you didn't have the desire for it

Have you had any of these thoughts? If so, here's your proof that you are not alone.

You may feel overwhelmed by prayer, but be assured, God has made a way for us. Romans 8:26 (ESV) tells us, "Likewise the Spirit helps us in our weakness. For we do not know what to pray for as we ought, but the Spirit himself intercedes for us with groanings too deep for words."

God has provided His spirit to lead us, and He has also given us the Lord's Prayer as a model for prayer. Growing up in the church, you can hear some concepts so much that you eventually tune them out. Not on purpose. It just happens. One of these for me was that prayer was made up of four different parts. I was reminded of this when reading Keller's book. He studies and talks about complex concepts, and here he was referencing something I learned in middle school and kind of wrote off as elementary. He noted that the four traditional parts of a prayer are: 1. adoration 2. confession 3. supplication 4. thanksgiving. "We must know the awe of praising his glory, the intimacy of finding his grace, and the struggle of asking his help, all of which can lead us to know the spiritual reality of his presence."

Hearing this forced me to realize that my prayers have become a lot less adoration and confession and a lot more asking for things and thanking Him for things; it's a part of it but not the whole. Let's go over the four parts.

ADORATION

Prayers of adoration simply mean praising God for who He is, not what He has given. I can't think of a better way to begin a prayer than acknowledging why God is so worthy of being glorified in this manner. If there were no reason to praise Him, we could end this whole prayer thing here, but, y'all, He is so worthy. This prepares our hearts so beautifully and puts us in a place of realizing the power He has in the following three parts.

Studying the Bible goes hand in hand with this because as we read, we learn all about His character. Commit to learning the character of God through His Word, and if you are unsure of where to start, I love how Psalm 145 describes His nature. Worship songs are also a great example of prayers of adoration, so feel free to belt it out to open a prayer.

CONFESSION

As I went through a study during Lent, I realized how much confession was lacking in my life. I regularly thought about my sins but usually more so in a "Darn it! I can't believe I did that!" sort of way. God desires for me to acknowledge my sins and lay them at the cross knowing He already died for all the sins of the world—the ones that came before His death and the ones that would come after.

When we don't confess our sins, we create a barrier between us and God. We don't lose salvation, but we hinder our fellowship with Him. If you are feeling particularly distant from God, search your heart and see if there is any sin that hasn't been brought to light yet. And be on the lookout for pride. It can get in the way of confession because we are constantly looking for excuses for our choices and behavior. Ask for humility and an open heart to accept the truth. Some sins we are not even aware of, so this open heart makes a way for Him to show us.

SUPPLICATION

This is the part of the prayer where we share our requests with the Lord. I think the progression of the other two parts to get here is powerful: we first acknowledge God's power and second humble ourselves knowing how much we need Him. A humble heart that prays expectantly to a mighty God is the perfect way to approach the throne of God with our requests. It also keeps us from treating prayer like a genie in a lamp.

This is something I have totally done by the way. I remember praying for a car. It was a hunter green Saturn, to be exact, and I was twelve years old. I remember sitting in my room thinking, *If I believe, it will happen. God will give me this car.* I must have overheard John 14:13 that says, "If you ask Me anything in My name, I will do it." My ESV commentary notes for this verse say, "Praying in Jesus' name means praying in a way consistent with his character and his will . . . Effective prayer must ask for and desire what Jesus delights in." How often do our prayers match the desires of the Lord? How often do they contradict them? Are we really surprised when prayers don't get answered the way we want when they are so far from God's intent for us?

Psalm 37:4 says, "Delight yourself in the Lord, and he will give you the desires of your heart."

What does it mean to practically delight in the Lord? To find delight in Him. To do this, I think we have to learn His character and spend time in His presence. I think when we learn His character and appreciate His massiveness, we bend our will to His with the understanding that our desires are better left in His hands to do what He wills. His will doesn't bend to us. When hearts are changed, desires change too.

THANKSGIVING

The final part is thanking God for all the blessings He has given us. We will discuss this so much more in the chapter on joy, but for now, I'll simply say, this is the start of joy. Thanksgiving isn't some fluffy optional part of prayer. It's essential. To pray prayers of thanksgiving, our eyes have to be wide open to see all those blessings in our lives. Every morning I pray and ask God to give me eyes to see every blessing. There are days I don't pray that. I can have the exact same set of events but a totally different response: one that is self-focused and ungrateful. It's an essential way to end a prayer. Thanksgiving sets up our whole day with a fresh perspective.

What a beautiful progression for our prayers. Not every prayer we offer to the Lord needs to follow this, or any, specific format but I would encourage you to dig deep and see if any part has been missing in your prayers like confession and adoration have been from mine.

Maybe you have been a Christian for a while and you are comfortable with prayer, but you simply don't make the time to do it. I think part of the reason why is we like instant gratification, and prayer is rarely that. As we open our eyes, our world normally looks exactly the same as before we prayed, and the silence can make us feel unheard. It takes time and patience, but the benefits are rich beyond anything we could hope for. I experience a few different things as a result of my time in prayer:

1. My heart is changed. I think we can get caught up more in how our circumstances are changed as we pray, but I tend to see more change in my heart than anything else. When I quiet my mind and all the things that need my attention so I can pray, I am able to dwell on the truth that I can so easily forget. I remember that God is a God worthy of my praise. That He is all-powerful and in control. I remember that the whole reason I am coming to Him in prayer is because I know He is worthy of it all.

2. My perspective is changed. Sometimes I initially start to pray asking for something I want that I know doesn't line up with God's plan. The very act of bowing my head to pray is a physical reminder that I want to bend my will to God's will, that I want God's desires to be my desires. The prayer I had planned to pray, *Lord make this situation different/better*, turns into, *Lord, your will be done. Carry me through this.* I seek less to get out of something and more to have Him go through it with me. I know challenges have a purpose, but until I'm speaking with this great God of mine, I let little things keep me from remembering this.

3. My circumstances are changed. This is the one we think we want to happen when we start praying. Even when things don't go the way I pray, I see my circumstances change, and I know it is because God's hand is in them. Those seemingly unanswered prayers ARE answered. When I have spent a whole month on my knees praying to the Lord for something and His response is different than my request, I feel all the more confident that God's will is being done. And when I have prayed for something and God answers in my favor, I am all the more confident that God's will is being done. Two different answers can have the same response from me when I know I have prayed about it.

Do you believe all these things could happen when you pray?

In *Prayers for the New Bride*, Jennifer White says, "If we ask God for His help and do not trust Him enough to do what He says, we should not expect to receive anything from Him. Asking and not acting lands us in the category of double-minded and unstable in all our ways" (James 1:6-8).

If you don't yet believe God is capable of answering your prayers, spend some time studying the promises He made in the

Bible. I would also challenge you to start a list of ways God has been faithful to you in the past. This is one thing I love about my prayer journal. When I have moments of doubt, I can look no further than the past two years of answered prayers and see that He has been at work. It's crazy how easily I forget.

And if we still have doubts, God wants to hear that too. David, whom God calls "a man after His own heart," cried out ugly tears and ugly prayers in Psalms. He was confused and didn't understand what God was doing but trusted Him anyway. It's refreshing to read David's messy and honest cries to the Lord and be reminded that God wants us to come to Him with it all.

The very act of praying can be such an elusive thing. There seem to be no boundaries for how they start and end, which makes it hard to stay focused. So many of you stated simple distractions like Netflix or the phone ringing or even the dog barking as things that kept you from prayer. I have an entire chapter on distractions that I hope will help, but here are a handful of tips that have helped me with creating boundaries for my prayers.

1. Make a commitment. Tell a friend. Put it on your calendar. Set your timer. Make it real. This is your prayer time. Otherwise, floating in and out of prayers is inevitable. This is not always a bad thing. God does ask us to pray without ceasing. This can look like a quick sentence or two throughout our day. But you also need time where God has your full, undivided attention.

2. Make it the first part of your day. Don't pick up the things that distract you until after you've had a little time in prayer. It is much easier to fight distractions *before* we are surrounded by them than after.

3. Walk and pray. When I was pregnant, I would walk around the lake by our apartment and pray for our little girl, my husband, my symptoms, our future, and my business goals. Now with Vivi, our walks are still my favorite prayer time. I set my journal up on her stroller canopy and just start praying. I think the momentum of walking and the energy that it provides help me keep praying. And my desire to keep praying helps me to keep walking. I also don't have all the distractions of home, and I can look up to the heavens and feel a closeness to God that I can't always feel under my roof.

4. Pray out loud. When we are in the car, especially when Vivi is with me, I love to pray. I can get so flustered by traffic or a fussy back-seat driver. Praying calms us both down. My out-loud prayers seem to be the most honest and child-like. My words don't come out perfect. I'll say something that I mean but wish I could take back, but it's out there and I'm given the chance to acknowledge my true feelings instead of hiding behind pomp and circumstance. Praying out loud means we are not only saying the words, but hearing them as well, which helps so much when it comes to our focus. And if you are uncomfortable praying in front of others, praying out loud alone will stretch this muscle.

5. Write down your prayers. Like praying out loud reinforces our focus, if you are saying it in your mind and then seeing it on paper, there is a greater chance of not getting distracted. Share your heart with the Lord like you would write a letter to a friend. It's simple and practical, but it can help.

6. Use a prayer journal. Before I designed the prayer journals, I would keep my prayers in a moleskin journal. This was fine, but I never kept up with it. Being the organization-loving girl I am, having a tool that made it easy for me to keep things straight AND had monthly sections helped me to make it a real habit instead of an occasional thing. My journal is always with me and I can pray in the car, in a line, everywhere.

7. When the words won't come, ask someone to pray with you. There have been so many moments in my life where I was too distracted or overwhelmed for words to come even when I wanted them to. Ask someone to pray with you. Hearing and believing their words is a powerful thing that draws us close to Him when we feel like it's impossible.

If you change one thing after reading this book, I hope it is regularly communicating with God. And with that, you will have knocked over the domino that can begin knocking over the rest.

H O M E W O R K

WORK IT OUT

Grab your *Lessons from The Finishing School* workbook
or your worksheet, A GUIDE TO PRAYER,
from the website and let the refining begin!

RECOMMENDED RESOURCES

A PRAYING LIFE
book by paul e. miller

PRAYER
book by timothy keller

VMP PRAYER JOURNAL
guided prayer journal - valmariepaper.com

VMP CONVERSATIONS JOURNAL
lined journal - valmariepaper.com

Find links to the worksheet and extra resources at
VALMARIEPAPER.COM/HOMEWORK
password: fairlady

3

The Good, Good Book

A GUIDE TO BIBLE STUDY

I love books. I learn a ton from them. It's why you are reading this book right now. No matter how good the book, though, none compare to the Word. A few months back, I was waiting somewhere and had about fifteen minutes to read. I was looking at my Kindle app with the latest business book I was reading and my Bible app. I remember thinking to myself, "I'll read the book since it will change my business." I cringe thinking I ever thought that even for a moment. Once the thought finished, I realized just how ridiculous that sounded. I had placed a higher value on a business book to change me then than the Word.

I think this is part of the struggle of making time with our Bibles. We forget its potency. I just stopped to make sure potency was the right word to use here, and I think God *may* be trying to tell me something. Dictionary.com says it means "power; authority; effectiveness; strength; capacity to be, become or develop; potentiality; a person or thing exerting power or influence."

Could we tattoo on our foreheads that the Bible is potent? It's all these things. It is power and authority. It is effective and strong. It has the capacity to develop ME, and it has power and influence. If I lived my life constantly knowing this about the Bible, I doubt it would take much convincing to pick it up to read.

I love what Jen Hatmaker says in her book 7. "The careful study of the Word has a goal, which is not the careful study of the Word. The objective is to discover Jesus and allow Him to change our trajectory. Meaning, a genuine study of the Word results in believers who feed poor people and open up their guest rooms; they're adopting and sharing, mentoring and intervening."

Studying the Bible shouldn't end when we close the book. It should transform our actions. It's our handbook for life. 2 Timothy 3:16-17 (NASB) says, "All Scripture is inspired by God and profitable for teaching, for reproof, for correction, for training in righteousness; so that the man of God may be adequate, equipped for every good work."

If it is not transforming our lives, how is it any better than the fiction novels we read for enjoyment that have no bearing on who we become?

Would you ever value your favorite beach read the way you would the Bible? The Sunday school answer is no. But if the Word is not transforming us, doesn't it carry the same value as a book we enjoy reading but forget about once we turn the last page? That is a pretty harsh reality, but when I think of this in my own life, it reminds me how valuable the Word is and how much I am missing out on when I treat it like anything less than the truth God wrote for us to read.

So we know the Word is powerful. Why, then, do so many of us say we don't feel God speak to us when we read? I started reading *Women of the Word* by Jen Wilkin and was amazed how backward I had been approaching the Bible and how this might be a reason we struggle to hear God speak through His Word. I had come to the Bible asking questions like, "What does this say about me or mean for my life?" when I should have been asking, "What does this say about God?"

Jen says, "We ask [the Bible] to tell us about ourselves, and all the while it is telling us about 'I AM.' We think that if it would just tell us who we are and what we should do, then our insecurities, fears, and doubts can never be banished by the knowledge of who we are. They can only be banished by the knowledge of 'I AM.'"

The New Living Translation of John 5:39 illustrates this quite succinctly. "You search the Scriptures because you think they give you eternal life. But the Scriptures point to me!"

As I have let this thought sink in, it has changed my approach to Bible reading and added to my joy in the process. I am much more expectant when I read the Word to see more of who God is and less focused on myself. God still teaches me so much about me in His Word, but it is a beautiful by-product of opening my Bible and looking for God instead of my own needs.

I also realize I make the Bible about me in other ways too. There are books in the Bible I totally neglect because they seem boring (Numbers) or scary (Revelation). Recently, I read Revelations and realized what an incredible book it was. It is such a testament to the bigness of God that I can sometimes forget as I pick and choose passages to read.

Maybe I am not hearing God because I expect Him to speak to my heart, when He is actually speaking to my mind. Jen quoted Paul Bloom, a Yale professor: "People ask me, 'How do you get more pleasure out of life?' And my answer is extremely pedantic: Study more . . . The key to enjoying wine isn't just to guzzle a lot of expensive wine, it's to learn about wine."

This makes sense to me with hobbies. If you are more invested in a team, you will appreciate it more than watching two teams you have no clue about. If you learn how to play the guitar, you will enjoy it more than if you just picked it up and tried to play it.

For the Bible to become real to us, it requires more than just clocking mindless hours. Reading requires our mind. We need to dig into the Word. Then we need to dig some more. The meat of the Scripture isn't at surface level. Fred Craddock said, "Some truths are not available to the casual passerby." A casual reader won't be looking for it like a serious student will. We might find a nice quote that makes us feel good when we glaze through a passage, but if we hope for more from our reading, we have to be intentional.

We can walk away with more than just a verse that makes us smile. We can be transformed by the knowledge in the Word and learn who God is and how it applies to our life. He literally says in His Word that if we seek wisdom, we will find it.

My son, if you will receive my words and treasure my commandments within you, make your ear attentive to wisdom, incline your heart to understanding; for if you cry for discernment, lift your voice for understanding; if you seek her as silver and search for her as for hidden treasures; Then you will discern the fear of the Lord and discover the knowledge of God. For the Lord gives wisdom; from His mouth come knowledge and understanding. - Proverbs 2: 1-6 (NASB)

It is in the discovery of who God is that I am refined and challenged to look more and more like Him. As I see His faithfulness, I can then trust what His Word means for me.

As I've written this book, I have realized just how often I need to seek God's truth on a thousand different things. So many times I found myself thinking, "What does God say about this?" It's been such a fruit-filled time and has me wanting to keep asking this question.

When you have a question and aren't sure what to think, maybe instead of saying "just Google it" we can say "look it up in your Bible." Psalm 119:105 says, "Your word is a lamp for my feet, a light on my path." Are we letting the Word illuminate our path? Some days, I hold my Bible and I am amazed by what I'm holding in my hands. It is full of things that will direct my steps and lead me to the Lord if I take the time to read.

Other days, I'd read a great passage and think about how it applies to me, jot down a note, and move on with my day. But I want the Word to wash over me. I want my voice to be covered in the saltiness of the Word instead of an outflow of me alone. You may study and read something that doesn't seem to apply to you at the moment, but it goes into your thought bank. How sweet to recall a passage you read months earlier "for such a time as this."

You might have had someone in your life like I did who always had a Scripture to share whenever you talked to them. This was my mom, and in my youth, it was actually pretty annoying. Why did she have to turn everything into a "teachable moment"? Now I have a much deeper appreciation for her quickness to turn to the Bible, because that's where I want my truth coming from, not the world.

It is imperative that we prepare our minds each day before we head out into a world that is filled with opportunities to love others and to glorify God as well as opportunities to choose selfishness and a host of other qualities that don't glorify God.

The Bible can be an overwhelming book, but I think when we sit down and diligently pursue wisdom as we read, God will reveal His truth. Some things will require brave questions and more research. There are tons of passages that initially have me scratching my head. A quote I read from Shelene Bryan in *Love, Skip, Jump* steps on my toes as I come up with every excuse to not pursue God: "In the presence of this massive God, you suddenly realize how foolish you have been to give so little of your attention, how foolish everyone has been to virtually ignore Him."

When we get to heaven and see the fullness of His glory, I don't want to kick myself for thinking how pointless it was that I skipped my time reading the Bible to finish a few more emails. We can get a glimpse of His glory here on earth, and the Word is our window. It's also what gives us perspective to see all the world around us through God's eyes. My days are vastly different when I see people the way God sees them rather than how I want to see them.

Here are a few tips to help inspire consistent, intentional time reading the Bible:

1. Set up a time. If we don't plan a time, it won't happen. Simple as that. If you say you are too busy, reevaluate where you are spending your time and make this happen. I wake up at 5:00 every morning. I'm no saint. I just know without my time in the Word and praying, my center of gravity shifts from God to me, and this totally affects my juggling of mom, wife, and business owner. Because of this, I prioritize it and a busy day can wait.

2. Set up a place. Have a designated spot for reading. It might be the couch, the bed, or a special chair. Create a cozy spot and even some things that signal that this is Bible time, not checking emails time. Every night, I set up my spot with a certain blanket and my tray with my Bible, prayer journal, gratitude journal, and note-taking journal. When I roll out of bed super early, everything is ready for me.

3. Have a plan before you sit down. We are lazy people. And if we don't have a game plan or know what we will read, it takes that much more energy to do it. It's just one more obstacle standing between us and actually reading. If you need to, plan this monthly or just decide which book of the Bible you will read next ahead of time. I have spent full "Bible reading sessions" simply flipping through trying to figure out what to read next.

4. Read with expectancy. I have already mentioned how potent the Word is. What would happen if we read in light of that? If we aren't looking for God to work through His Word, we will miss it. We have to be diligent. I love what Proverbs 21:5 says. "The plans of the diligent lead surely to abundance, but everyone who is hasty comes only to poverty." We know when the Bible talks about poverty and abundance, it is not just talking about money. What about abundance in truth and knowledge? When we read hastily to simply check it off our list, we aren't reaping that abundance.

5. Utilize resources. Read different translations and read the verses that are cross-referenced at the bottom of the page or in the margins. This is part of the digging. As you come at a passage from all angles, a certain word may spark something for you. Use a commentary as well. They can help provide contextual information that can sometimes get lost because we live in a different cultural time. I recommend the ESV Study Bible. There are tons of different versions, but mine is white, black, and red with a hard covering. It actually reminds me of a textbook, which just reminds me I'm always a student of the Word.

H O M E W O R K

WORK IT OUT

Grab your *Lessons from The Finishing School* workbook
or your worksheet, A GUIDE TO BIBLE STUDY,
from the website and let the refining begin!

RECOMMENDED RESOURCES

ESV STUDY BIBLE

JOURNALING BIBLE

GIVE ME JESUS JOURNAL
quiet time journal - lifelivedbeautifully.com

Find links to the worksheet and extra resources at
VALMARIEPAPER.COM/HOMEWORK
password: fairlady

4

Goal #2: Be Weird

A G U I D E T O G O A L S

In elementary school, before entering a new grade, I'd make a list of goals of things I wanted to do for the upcoming school year. They were simple things like make good grades, be a good friend, and one year, in complete confidence in my own skin, I said I wanted to be "weird." I WANTED TO BE WEIRD. This still cracks me up to think about. Grown-up and sometimes insecure Valerie is super impressed that I was willing to be different and even made it a goal of mine. Looking back on pictures and reading the crazy poems and songs I wrote as a kid, it is safe to say I accomplished my goal better than I ever could have imagined. Just overachieving as usual.

It is twenty years later, and I still get all giddy inside to start a new sheet of paper and write out goals for the year. But nowadays, I'm looking to include God in this process. It sounds simple enough. God is a part of every area of my life. Why would I not include Him in shaping my dreams for life?

It can be more complicated than I think. I have trouble reconciling goals here on earth with God's plan for my life. I don't want to become legalistic in my relationship with Him or take control, but I also don't want to kick my shoes off and get lazy waiting for God to drop a purposeful life at my door.

In comes 1 Kings 5–6, which is all about Solomon building the temple. What struck me about this passage was how overwhelming of a project this seemed to be and how wisely and swiftly Solomon seemed to handle things. He simply made a plan and made it happen. He was the project manager for the temple, something with a legacy that has lasted far beyond his lifetime. Here are four lessons I learned from Solomon: 1. Seek wisdom. 2. Make a plan. 3. Act on it. 4. Complete it. These are pretty basic, right? But what if Solomon hadn't asked for wisdom? Would he have known how to negotiate with the Hiram, King of Tyre, for cedar? Or known the right amount of men to put on the task? Or what if he didn't make a plan? Would the king of Tyre have even listened to him at all? Or what if he didn't act on it? What good would the perfect plan be that isn't actually put in motion? What good would a half-complete temple have been? And how would that have changed the generations to come?

Let's look at those 4 lessons closer.

1. Seek wisdom. This is huge. Without it, we could end up in the completely wrong place. Indulge me as I use the classic plane analogy. A plane that is even one degree off course will continue moving that direction and be taken farther and farther off the path—not one mile but hundreds of miles. Our starting point is very important, but the direction we head is even more so. Ask God what His plan for you is and seek it out. How do you seek it out? Soak your mind in His Word, seek wise counsel from trusted believers, and devote yourself to lots of prayer. I have also fasted during periods of decision and experienced God's truth in a unique way. Be quiet enough to hear God's nudging. I remember when this idea really hit me. I prayed and prayed God would speak to me and felt like He was ignoring my request, but the truth was my communication with Him was limited to me talking. That's it. No actual listening on my part. Very rarely will you hear a horn blow announcing God's plan or see it written in the sky, so quiet your mind enough to be able to hear Him. For me recently, this meant shutting off the phone and computer for a short period of time to reduce the noise of the world around me.

2. Make a plan. I have used Lara Casey's Powersheets for two years and can easily say my life has been much more intentional than ever before, and I have accomplished so many of my goals. I highly recommend using them and will include a link to them at the end of the chapter. Writing out our goals makes them real. It might sound overly simple, but it's true. Until we know what we are going after, it's just an idea. And until we have a plan in action, it's just a dream. I have done this with tons of things. I'll think, "Oh I'd like to fast today from _____" and two hours later when I'm frustrated and need _____, I blow off my original plan because it wasn't *technically* a plan. It was just a thought that popped in that I never really committed to. Even better, share it with someone so you have the accountability. On my blog, I share my goals each month. It has been the best accountability and helps me sidestep the whole "not technically a plan" excuse.

3. Act on it. So you've made your plan. Now it's time to step out in obedience. You have heard from the Lord and are in line with His will. Sometimes the first step is hardest. I break down each of my goals into action steps. Each week, I try to add some of these steps to my week. If they are not on my calendar, the urgent but less important things will crowd out my goals. If we aren't spending our days working on our big goals, we can't make them happen. Part of acting involves self-control and creating good habits and routines, all of which we will talk about soon!

What if you don't feel like you have heard Him clearly? Keep asking Him to speak and give Him plenty of space to talk. Then take the first step of where you feel like God is leading you. If it's wrong and you are tuned in to Him, you will feel an uneasiness or lack of peace. 1 Corinthians 14:33a (ESV) says, "For God is not a God of confusion but of peace." And remember that God's plan will not contradict His Word, so keep soaking up the truth from the Bible so you can determine if it does.

4. Complete it. Isn't this basically like act on it? Here's the difference. We can be really good at starting something but really bad at completing it. We get bored, or something shiny and new comes along that captures our attention. Solomon was a great example of completing something. He built a temple, y'all! Can you imagine that thing half finished? It would be pretty useless. Completing is a test of our patience and endurance and a true faith builder. God is all over this goal thing and will transform us through this process. One thing that I do to keep focused on my goals so that I see it through to completion is to pair verses with each goal. Once the goals are made, I choose several verses from the Bible to pair with each one. I use a concordance and search for words on the topic or search other resources or books that talk about the topic. I write each verse out on notecards so I can remind myself of God's truth in my plans for the year. I have a reminder on my phone to read Scripture each night before bed and read these often. It helps me to not lose sight of my goals and keeps them a priority so that I can finish strong.

I do have one *kind of* big caveat to this whole goal thing. Leave room for God to work and for the right opportunities. How many of your favorite memories of the last year were not even part of your goal list? Probably a decent amount. Here is where "trying to control my future" and "sitting back and waiting for God to do all the work" balance each other. Set a plan, but keep your hands open instead of clinching your fist and being unwilling to part with a goal. Proverbs 16:9 (ESV) tells us, "The heart of man plans his way, but the Lord establishes his steps." Part of me is more excited for what is not on my goals list knowing God will bring things my way as I open my heart to his plan.

The practical way I "keep my heart open" is I pray about each of my goals. Each month, I include my goals in my personal section of my prayer journal. Each day, I am bringing my plan to the Lord and giving it up to Him to do His will. A perfect example. This book was NOT a part of my goals, but God is already bringing new dreams my way.

What are your lifelong dreams? And what are you doing this very day to make those happen? One of my very favorite quotes by John C. Maxwell is, "We overexaggerate yesterday, we overestimate tomorrow and we underestimate today." Let that truth sink in. So much of why we stay stuck boils down to our ideas about our days. Whether it's successes or failures from yesterday, we let them distract us from the present. Our failures distract us for obvious reasons, but even our successes can stall us if we focus on them so much that we miss the potential for today. All I can picture is Uncle Rico from *Napoleon Dynamite* reveling in the glory days of a high school championship. He's got to be in his forties with nothing left to show but an achievement from high school. I don't know about y'all, but that sounds like a fruit that has shriveled up.

On the other hand, we build up the potential of tomorrow envisioning the willpower we will suddenly possess and the fantasy that tomorrow it will be easier to tackle. Aren't we all starting our diet on Monday? Seriously, a Monday? Aren't Mondays already kind of a challenge? The fact that we even think we will attempt a diet starting on a Monday shows what a fantasy we have built around tomorrow and beyond. After marinating on these truths the last few weeks, I have started to notice how often this thinking, even subconsciously, affects me.

Lastly, we don't value today. We see it as small and meaningless in the grand scheme of things, but all we have is a series of todays, and we have to act now. The past will always be the past, the future will always be the future, and today will always be the day we have to work with and make our God-sized dreams come true. The Lord has great plans for your life, and today is the perfect day to say yes to them.

H O M E W O R K

WORK IT OUT

Grab your *Lessons from The Finishing School* workbook
or your worksheet, A GUIDE TO GOALS,
from the website and let the refining begin!

RECOMMENDED RESOURCES

TODAY MATTERS
book by john c. maxwell

MAKE IT HAPPEN
book by lara casey

POWERSHEETS
goal-setting worksheets - laracaseyshop.com

Find links to the worksheet and extra resources at
VALMARIEPAPER.COM/HOMEWORK
password: fairlady

What I Gave Up for Lent

A GUIDE TO DISTRACTIONS

Can you imagine what your life would be like without all the distractions that seem to hinder us from what matters most? What would you accomplish? What new things would you enjoy?

You have already made some God-centered goals for your life. If we lived in our fairytale land, they would probably all have a nice little check mark next to them. Instead, we live in a world with distractions at every turn. They seem to be such a source of frustration for so many of us. They are so insignificant yet hold us back from a rich, full life.

Americans watch almost thirty hours of TV a week. This sounded absolutely crazy to me, but when I added up my own average TV watching, it wasn't that far off, especially if you include those times when the TV is on in the background just for the noise.

Being a work-at-home mom can mean very little adult interaction. I used to work for a newspaper with maybe fifty cubicles all around. I had interaction. Then when I was a wedding planner, I shared a workspace with two other creatives. We all had our individual offices but talked throughout the day, and I met with brides and vendors every day. Now it's just me and Vivi most days from 7-6, and there is no sweeter sound than the TV humming to keep me company. Or so I thought. What started out as a little background noise became me turning the TV on every time Vivi would go to sleep and it staying on during our lunch and into the afternoon.

It had become mindless as many distractions are. Laura Vanderkam wrote a wonderful book, *168 Hours*, on how we spend our time and how we have plenty of it if we use it correctly. She said, "We don't think about how we want to spend our time, and so we spend massive amounts of time on things—television, Web surfing, housework, errands—that give a slight amount of pleasure or feeling of accomplishment, but do little for our careers, our families, or our personal lives. We spend very little time on things that require more thought or initiative, like nurturing our kids, exercising, or engaging in the limited hours we do work in deliberate practice of our professional crafts. We try to squeeze these high-impact activities around the edges of things that are easy, or that seem inevitable merely because we always do them or because we think others expect us to."

I have definitely been guilty of squeezing in the important around the easy and not so important. This truth stung as I saw the repercussions of this in my life. So for Lent this year, I decided to give up TV for the work day, and it has been the most incredible blessing. I had no idea how much of a distraction it had become. I had gotten used to procrastinating things like blogging or tough emails until I had time to think clearly. Honestly, I'm not sure you would have this book in your hands if I hadn't given it up.

When the idea first popped into my head to give up TV for Lent, I was thinking through how many days that is and how it would be impossible. I really didn't see myself being able to do it. Forty days is a long time. A week would have been a long time. But I felt strongly that God wanted me to do it. I had to journal about my decision to do it just so I couldn't say later that I really didn't mean it.

The first few days were hard. It was a habit, and I didn't know what to do without my little comfort. By the end, I didn't have a desire for it at all and plan on keeping this a habit for life.

I hate that something like screens can keep me from the important things in my life. TV is not important. I'm not saying it's the devil, but let's call it what it is. TV will not help you do what matters. I love my Netflix and can binge on a series as much as the next girl, but if I keep pretending and don't acknowledge that it has no value compared to a night reading a good book in the bath or talking with my husband or serving at my church, why would I ever choose the latter? I need to make this realization in my life so that I can slowly change my desire and my habits.

I remember when my mom went to Haiti for the first time. I was eleven years old, and I remember three things from her trip: 1. While she was serving the poor, our brand-new sofas had come in. They were the perfect shade of dirt and beige and mauve to hide all the stains we were about to unleash on it. 2. She brought back my brother this toy bus made out of wood. I thought she should have saved her $0.40 and got him the real deal from Toys R' Us. 3. She said the people were there were happier than she ever expected.

Luckily, that last one has impacted me the most. It stuck because I just couldn't understand it. These people were not just poor, they were really poor. What did they have to be happy about? They sat in four-hour church services in a hot building, had to labor for their meals, and were woken at night by creepy crawly tarantulas. This was not my idea of happy. My mom told me it was because they had a heavenly perspective. She said so many of their songs are all about heaven. They aren't distracted by the temporary like we are, and although they have a million obstacles for their happiness, their joy overflows wildly because they are focused on what actually matters.

I kind of just assumed people from poor countries were jealous of the American Dream, and maybe some are, but there they were happier than I'd consider most Americans. It makes sense. We have a ton of less important things that clamor for that number-one spot in our hearts.

What's clamoring for your number-one spot? What are your distractions? Be honest here. You don't need to ban them from your life, but bringing them to light *will* help you start seeing them differently. An eye-opening experiment that will help you see what your distractors are is tracking your time for a week. I did this when reading *168 Hours*. Tracking every little thing you do will probably surprise you. You may notice where a little more focus and less distractions could give you time for all those things you say you don't have time for right now.

If you aren't comfortable talking to yourself, this one may be a little out there for you, but what if when you sit down to do something you really need to focus on, you simply state the facts. 1. What you need to do with your time. 2. What you do not need to do with your time. 3. What the benefits will be if you choose both wisely.

An example from my life: "I am sitting down to read my Bible because it's vital to my daily life. I want to be changed by it, and I choose right now not to let social media or my to-do list distract me." Another example. "I am turning on my computer to answer client emails. I am not getting on to surf the web or online shop. If I use my time diligently now while I work, I can take Vivi to the zoo instead of having to attempt to work this afternoon while she plays."

Speaking it out loud makes it all the more real *and* realistic that it will actually happen. Too many times I am swayed by things simply because I didn't clearly define my boundaries. *Well techni-*

cally I didn't say I was going to work right now, so gap.com it is!

Sometimes what distracts us most are our very own thoughts. If this is the case for you, I highly recommend setting a timer for five minutes and emptying out everything on your mind before you sit down to work, pray, or play. Once you have it on paper, you don't have to loop it in your brain out of fear that you will forget it. This happens to me so often. My brain will not stop looping a thought until it is safely tucked away on my calendar or to-do list. Ideally we could just let it go, but this is hard. If something is distracting you, write it down and move on.

I have already mentioned, I'm not sure you would be reading this book if I hadn't given up TV for Lent. The reality of that is heavy. Our distractions don't just keep us from a productive day. They can also hinder us from something the Lord is calling us to do. He wants to use us, but how many of us are simply "too busy"? I'm using quotes, because if we cut out a few of our silly distractions, we'd no doubt have the time.

Satan could not be more thrilled when we get wrapped up in worldly things and lose focus on our purpose. It's just one more obstacle as we try to live a fruit-filled life that glorifies God and is one more way we stay attached to our temporary kingdom on earth.

If he finds a good distraction that works for you, he will keep going back to the same barrel. He is not creative. Is there one distraction that you struggle with rejecting the most? Listen to the thoughts that come into your head when you have the urge to succumb to your distractions. Are there any lies you are believing? What do you tell yourself are the benefits of giving into your distractions? Identifying these things are the keys to changing it. What truth do you need to speak? Study what the Bible has to say about related topics.

Hebrews 12:1-2 is my theme verse when it comes to distractions. Write it on a note card and memorize it. When temptation comes, speak this out loud and turn away from the distraction.

> Therefore, since we are surrounded by such a great cloud of witnesses, let us throw off everything that hinders and the sin that so easily entangles. And let us run with perseverance the race marked out for us, fixing our eyes on Jesus, the pioneer and perfecter of faith. For the joy set before him he endured the cross, scorning its shame, and sat down at the right hand of the throne of God.

This idea of fixing our eyes on Jesus, throwing off everything that tries to slow us down, and running hard after Him makes me tear up to imagine. I want to live free from the commotion of this world and not let some semblance of life just happen to me. I want to run the race that God has for me.

You might feel like this is all overkill for something like checking Instagram too much, but living an intentional life does not happen by accident. It requires our diligence—our saying no to things that don't matter and saying yes to the things that do matter.

My quintessential writing spot has been our screened-in porch. It's the perfect mix of quiet but not too quiet. No technology to distract me. No dishes or laundry to see in my peripheral. Just the hum from the birds that provide a steady rhythm to type. I got rid of those things that normally create noise in my head when looking for clarity. And so much happens in those moments that would have never happened if I been cavalier to think the distractions were not affecting me. Choosing to say no to them is hard, and I fail a lot at this. But when I get more and more glimpses of this intentional life, I know it's more than worth the sacrifice.

Here are a few practical tips to help get rid of distractions:

1. Name them. You won't know what to resist if you don't know what they are.

2. Identify the lie. Figure out what you are believing and the reason you keep letting them in.

3. Get rid of them. I literally have to delete Instagram off my phone every weekend or else I will mindlessly click on it. Sometimes our best of intentions are derailed by bad habits. We don't even choose it consciously.

4. State the benefits of getting rid of distractions. Laura says, "When you turn off the TV at night in order to talk with your partner, you will sleep better. When you sleep better, you'll be more focused at work. When you're focused at work, you will get more done in less time and get home earlier, you'll have more energy to play with your kids. When you've having fun with your kids, TV will seem a lot less interesting. And so the cycle repeats itself, until finally the life you want is there in the 168 hours you've got."

HOMEWORK

WORK IT OUT

Grab your *Lessons from The Finishing School* workbook
or your worksheet, A GUIDE TO DISTRACTIONS,
from the website and let the refining begin!

RECOMMENDED RESOURCES

168 HOURS
book by laura vanderkam

Find links to the worksheet and extra resources at
VALMARIEPAPER. COM/HOMEWORK.
password: fairlady

6

Half a Bag of Powdered Donuts

A GUIDE TO SELF-CONTROL

I didn't really realize I had a problem with self-control until I looked down and saw a half-eaten bag of powdered donuts that were supposed to be for a party I was throwing that night. I managed to eat *half a bag of powdered donuts* without even noticing. That takes an unabashed lack of self-control, friends. I thought for vanity's sake I should change it to maybe a handful of donuts or a quarter of the bag or maybe say the bag was actually pretty small, because surely the lesson can be learned with a less embarrassing picture, but no. *Half a bag of powdered donuts.* Isn't the first step to learning self-control or managing addictions admitting there is a problem? A smaller amount could be justified a million ways, but *half a bag of powdered donuts* couldn't be justified. Except maybe if I were stranded on a desert island and hadn't eaten for days. But there was no island. Just a refrigerator of fruits and veggies that sat quietly tucked away while I unknowingly ate *half a bag of powdered donuts.*

This little scenario caught my attention. It started a whole chain of thoughts about how rarely I exercise self-control and how I don't even feel any remorse for it.

I started thinking of other areas of life where self-control has been nowhere to be found. Take shopping, for instance. For years, I would not go to the mall but would make a trip to the Banana Republic outlet a few times a year and buy anything I needed for the next season or two. It was nothing to drop $200-300, because I really didn't shop often. I also had a full-time job and no kids. But with the ease of online shopping, a new baby, and my love for laying on my couch, this became a serious problem. Not blow-through-our-savings kind of problems, but operating-without-my-brain problems. It became more frequent and mindless. I didn't even see it escalating.

For you, it may be how you indulge in gossip. You drop one backward comment and a whole conversation starts brewing about someone, secrets come out, and two hours later, you don't even know how it happened. Or maybe your kids were being extra whiny and annoying and your anger grew before you even had a chance to stop it. In all these scenarios, including mine, we do what we want. That's the short version. We simply do whatever the heck we want to do.

Self-control means not letting our feelings and emotions control our choices but being led by the Spirit to act. Unfortunately, my big revelation was not enough. I knew I wasn't going to "get this under control" in my own strength, and I surely wasn't going to do it just because I ate half a bag of powdered donuts. I needed more.

So I began my quest to understand and learn self-control and started like any credible writer does, with dictionary.com. The definition of self-control is "control or restraint of oneself or one's actions, feelings, etc." Self-control is basically thinking before I act and a fruit of the spirit that the Lord gives to believers.

My word for 2015, STEADFAST, is all wrapped up in self-control, though I never really thought about it until now. Funny how God will keep tapping on your shoulder with a point until you get it. Being steadfast is gaining self-control over our emotions, abiding in God's truth, and hopping off the roller coaster that we let dictate how we feel and thereby respond. Self-control in areas like food and spending happens when I remain steadfast in God's truth. When I listen to thoughts that say food will make me happy or spending will satisfy, I am believing lies and much more likely to not exercise self-control.

So who is supposed to be working on this self-control thing anyway? Is it all God? Is it all me? Who's doing the work? As I mentioned earlier, I simply have forgotten what self-control is and that it is important, but maybe another reason I don't exercise it is because I forget who makes this happen. I assume that the only way to change is through God, and this is true; but the part I always forget is that He gives me the tools, and I have the choice about whether I use them or not.

"For the Spirit God gave us does not make us timid, but gives us power, love and self-discipline." - 2 Timothy 1:7

"But the fruit of the Spirit is love, joy, peace, forbearance, kindness, goodness, faithfulness, gentleness and self-control." - Galatians 5:22-23a

Verses like these encourage me and remind me that I have been equipped by God to resist temptation. Striving for self-control without God remains a self-centered pursuit. It might look noble and like I'm trying hard, but the result doesn't glorify God; it glorifies myself.

In my research I found this great quote by David Mathis about the perspective we should have:

We want Jesus to get glory. We want to control ourselves in the power he supplies. We learn to say no, but we don't just say no. We admit the inadequacy, and emptiness, of doing it on our own. We pray for Jesus's help, secure accountability, and craft specific strategies.

That's a lot to take in. Did you know self-control to not eat all your kid's Halloween candy could be so spiritual? I didn't either. I see three points to help us work out this self-control thing.

1. Admit we cannot do this without Jesus. As I walk through this in my own life, it's interesting how the longer I am a Christian and the deeper I grow in my faith, the more I realize my need for Him and the areas of my life that are dark and dingy without His presence. It used to depress me to think about every time I noticed a new struggle in my life, but the truth is, the fact that we see more in our life shows that we are getting closer to Him. His light is what illuminates the dark places. Those who want to stay in sin and darkness don't get close enough to the light to draw any sort of attention to their problems. And if you can't see it, you can't change it.

2. Humbly come in prayer to the Lord. I think this does a few things. It's inviting the Lord to work in our life to change our circumstances or our perspective. It's putting us in a position to not stumble into pride thinking we can do it on our own and fall just as quickly. But even practically speaking, it's staying at the front of my mind. The things that show up in my prayers are the things I more intentionally give energy to. This leads to number three.

3. Know that there is a battle over our choices and be intentional to fight. Edward Welch wrote in *Self-Control: The Battle Against One More*, "As the Hebrews were promised the land, but had to take it by force, one town at a time, so we are promised the gift of self-control, yet we also must take it by force."

Does this fire anyone else up besides me? To hear that we have been promised this gift is incredibly motivating. It's ours for the taking. God doesn't say it will be easy or handed to us, but it is there for us. We don't have to wonder, "Am I going to work this hard and find out I will *never* have enough self-control to conquer this struggle?" The answer is, you *do* have enough self-control, so fight for it. It's His fruit, not ours. Our power will never be enough. By His grace, He gives us that spirit of self-control.

How do we acquire this gift of self-control? One town (or step) at a time. But what are we up against? As I mentioned before, we believe lies that tell us that the thing we want will satisfy us. The story is as old as time. Literally. Adam and Eve in the Garden of Eden were the first to try and fail at this, yet we keep thinking we will get a different response. That's our sinful flesh. We are not only working with our own sinful desires, but Satan doubles down on those things we already struggle with and makes sure they look enticing to us. These pleasures are so temporary, yet we can fall into the same thing over and over again. Part of this is habits, but part of this is thinking that once we get what we want, all will be perfect. And perfect is an illusion.

What if we could rationalize in a moment of intense temptation that the very pleasure we'd indulge in would be gone in a minute and we would be left feeling regretful? In our minds, we think indulging is a freeing act. That's why we do it. We don't like confinement. But here is a truth I never want to forget: there is FREEDOM in self-control. Proverbs 25:28 tells us, "Like a city whose walls are broken down is a man who lacks self-control." In biblical times, a city with no walls was wide open to enemies. It felt free, but it wasn't free at all. It was a terrifying and vulnerable way to live. Our self-control acts as a wall for us and protects us and gives us freedom too.

The Lord has been crying out to teach me this lesson, and I

have been listening half-way. I found notes I had written in the past on the Proverbs 25:28 passage from above and everything I learned while reading. I had included a few other areas where I lose self-control and even those things that tend to cause it:

1. cursing because of pressure
2. grumpy because of pain
3. selfish because of hurt feelings

These are all emotional responses to outer situations. Self-control is a response set apart from my emotions and instead is a response decided in advance based on a standard I live by.

What is my plan in advance? What is my standard? Just because I feel pressure or things don't go according to plan, does it really justify my lack of self-control? It is in these less-than-ideal situations that things normally fall apart. And even if I could justify it, it NEVER benefits myself, so it's silly to think that having a good reason to do it makes it worthwhile to do. More importantly, though, the Lord desires my steadfastness.

James 1:12,14 (ESV) says, "Blessed is the man who remains steadfast under trial, for when he has stood the test he will receive the crown of life, which God has promised to those who love Him... But each person is tempted when he is lured and enticed by his own design."

Self-control is important and so worth fighting for. And I am worth it. *You* are worth it. Without it, we become robots doing whatever our flesh tells us. With it, we see some of that fruit I can't stop yammering about.

HOMEWORK

WORK IT OUT

Grab your *Lessons from The Finishing School* workbook
or your worksheet, A GUIDE TO SELF-CONTROL,
from the website and let the refining begin!

RECOMMENDED RESOURCES

UNGLUED
book by lysa terkeurst

Find links to the worksheet and extra resources at
VALMARIEPAPER. COM/HOMEWORK.
password: fairlady

Cue the Chocolate

A GUIDE TO HABITS

In my research on self-control, I realized that so many things we do are automatic. We literally go on autopilot when we receive certain cues and act strictly out of habit. The key to change is breaking down and understanding the process of each habit to see what is triggering them and replace the habit with a new one that will bring about the same reward.

I was floored when I started looking at some of my habits. Like my dark chocolate obsession. I have been wanting to cut back because I eat way too many. While working through this, I realized I had gotten in a habit of putting Vivi to sleep for her nap, grabbing a handful of Hershey's dark chocolate, and heading to the couch to work. I would crave chocolate the instant I shut Vivi's door like Pavlov's dog.

I had no idea how much of a habit this had become although I had been doing it for weeks. I dissected it using some tools that I had learned from *The Power of Habit* by Jack D. Hodge, and this alone helped me to think before I acted and change my behavior.

Here was the pattern that Jack says every habit goes through:

1. The Trigger - The trigger is what puts me on autopilot.

Habits are mindless, and this is our cue to shut the brain off and do what autopilot knows to do. It is the initial signal to our brains that make us anticipate the reward and start the cycle to get there, and it doesn't even need my help to get this ball rolling. My trigger was when I put Vivi down to sleep and had alone time. I craved that feeling of "me time" or even just control after a morning of instructing and disciplining Vivi, being a short-order cook, a maid, and all the other sorts of things moms of toddlers can feel. This was my way of grabbing hold of me again.

2. The Process - The process is the step that takes us to the result. The key is not breaking this cycle all together. It's already ingrained in our brain. We simply have to change this portion of the cycle with a better process. For me, my process was grabbing chocolate and working from the couch. I decided that making a cup of my favorite tea and taking five minutes to stretch and pray before I started working would refresh me. Then I could sit at my desk, where I normally get more work done anyway, and have an intentional work session.

3. The Result - This is what we hope for the moment we hit autopilot. For me, it was feeling like I had a break and "me time." I had to realize that I could achieve this in healthy ways instead. Now when Vivi goes down to sleep, I know the "why" behind me choosing chocolate kisses, and this helps tremendously even if I don't stretch or pray. When I shut her bedroom door and think, *I'm craving chocolate all of sudden but I don't even think I want any,* I suddenly realize how mechanical my reaction has become.

Charles Duhigg in *The Power of Habit* (a different book!) says that as you begin trying to figure out new habits you want to create and bad habits to change, you should pick one keystone habit to focus on initially. This habit should be one that affects a multitude of areas. Cutting back on social media was my keystone. If I started my day without Instagram, I could jump right into my time with the Lord and maybe even have time to get a head start on emails before Vivi woke up. If I had my phone less with Vivi, I would enjoy her company more and invest in her growing to be a godly gal. If I had my phone less during my workday, I could complete my work sooner, leaving time to tidy the house before my husband got home and provide a place of peace. If I had my phone less in the evenings, I could have more real conversations and quality time, fostering my marriage. If I had my phone less before going to bed, I could go to sleep praying to the Lord instead of feeling the sense of comparison with others. If I had my phone less on the weekends, I could have more adventure.

That, my friends, is my keystone habit. Look at everything it changes. I enjoy social media and find a lot of real inspiration there from the people I follow. The time I spend there is meaningful, but when I spend a lot of time there, the benefits don't actually multiply, they just get muddled.

An example of other keystone habits may be starting the morning with lemon water or a workout or not turning on the TV until after work if you stay at home. The momentum this alone brings is crucial and so inspiring. Take the time to discover your keystone habit. The benefits will be exponential.

This principle of putting in the work to reap the reward is all over the Bible. Galatians 6:9 says, "Let us not become weary in doing good, for at the proper time we will reap a harvest if we do not give up." 1 Corinthians 15:58 says, "Therefore, my dear brothers and sisters, stand firm. Let nothing move you. Always give yourselves fully to the work of the Lord, because you know that your labor in the Lord is not in vain." Habits take steadfastness to develop them and perseverance to know it is worth it.

This stubborn gal wanted plenty of reinforcements, so I continued my research and was quickly reminded that it's what we do every day that matters instead of what we do every so often. If you work out regularly, you will see results eventually. It might take a while, but it will come. If you work out once a month and *don't* work out the other thirty times a month, what do you think the result will be? It's silly, but I expect the every-so-often accomplishment of a workout to transform me and get so frustrated when it doesn't. I forget what I'm doing (or not doing!) the other days of the week.

This is the whole message behind the book *The Compound Effect*. The author, Darren Hardy, mentions that the hardest part of doing the daily things is that results take a while, and most people aren't willing to commit to something without seeing more immediate results.

He says we stay enslaved to our bad habits because the consequences aren't immediate but the gratification of indulging is. "If that first forkful of cake instantly put fifty pounds on your frame, saying 'no thank you' to dessert would be the true piece of cake . . . Indulging in our bad habits doesn't seem to have any negative effects at all in the moment. But that doesn't mean you haven't activated the Compound Effect."

This imagery had me at cake. I love sweets and don't think a single cookie or two or four will make me gain weight. It's so small in the grand scheme of things, but it's the habit that's the problem. It's what happens over time. The compound effect is always at work either positively or negatively. We choose what effect it has on our life.

Once our habits or routines fall into a nice rhythm, it builds steam like a locomotive. Darren compares us to a parked train before we start practicing habits we want to implement. A single stick could stop a train that is not moving, but once that train starts moving, very little can stop it. Build momentum and work really hard to keep it going. It's easy to think that taking a week off only affects that week, but it means we've got to get our momentum going all over again, which is like pushing a train that is at a standstill.

As if what we have already mentioned isn't enough to convince us to change our habits, here's one more reason to hopefully seal the deal.

Besides being good to help us learn self-control in areas we are struggling with, Shawn Achor said in *The Happiness Advantage* that creating habits is great so that we can reserve our energy for big challenges. He said that we don't have an infinite amount of energy to be disciplined, so if we want to achieve in the big areas, we should reserve that energy for the biggest things. He even mentioned eating the same thing for breakfast every day just so there is one less decision to make. Are there areas that use so much of your energy that could be spent better somewhere else? The example that comes to my mind is my wardrobe. I spend about as much time committing to an outfit as some people spend picking a baby name. I'm exhausted before I even walk out of the door to tackle the day's agenda. What a defeated way to start.

Another way to approach changing habits is by putting obstacles in our way for habits we want to break and removing obstacles for habits we want to create. We all know this principle. It's why we lay our workout clothes out the night before or stock our refrigerator full of fruits and veggies at eye level. But how can this same principle work for those random habits that are specific to you?

I moved the chocolates from the cabinet that always gets opened to somewhere I'd have to go to specifically for them. Let's ask a tough question. Do you believe you can change? Do you believe that God can change you? Even scientists recognize that belief is needed for change to occur.

One thing I realized about my struggle to get fit was that I couldn't really visualize my body healthy and trim or active. Since high school, I have never lost any weight. I have slowly gained ten to fifteen pounds over ten years but not once lost the weight I wanted to lose. I realized this was a major factor in why I couldn't lose weight. I had never seen it happen, so I didn't believe I could. We have to transform our minds by truth because as we work to change our habits, every lie Satan can throw at us will tempt us.

Romans 12:2 sums this idea up so nicely. Keep it handy to remind yourself of God's truth when your flesh tries to tell you that change is impossible or at the very least, too hard and not worth doing.

Romans 12:2 says, "Do not conform to the pattern of this world, but be transformed by the renewing of your mind. Then you will be able to test and approve what God's will is – his good, pleasing and perfect will."

It is amazing the things God is teaching me as I write this book. I have been challenged so many times to live out exactly what I have learned and am sharing with you. There are moments of weakness where I still look so close to who I was before I learned what I'm sharing. Then there are moments of sweet victory, like the moment I am relishing in right now. I wanted to curl up on the couch with chocolates and forget about the laundry list of things I needed to do. Not to experience true rest but to simply be lazy because I deserved it. Saying I deserve something is usually enough to get me to indulge in anything. I am not a tough sell. But I kept thinking to myself, *Valerie, you are choosing not to do what you know you should do because it's hard right now. Your foot hurts, and it seems like the perfect excuse to veg out on the couch. But don't let your emotions drive you.* And y'all, I did what I needed to do and now I sit here on my bed typing with my dessert . . . two tangerines.

The funny thing is, I'm not relishing in the to-do list being done. I'm relishing in the strength I discovered about myself in the process. I consider myself pretty weak, and this gave me hope of God's power working in me and encouragement that I can choose the hard things. Who knew habits honored God? They can seem so legalistic and Pharisee-ish to me. The truth is, they reveal our fruit. We can *say* what we believe, but our actions tell others what we truly believe.

That is the beauty of habits. They give us opportunities to do the right thing well after our joy and motivation to do that thing has worn off. The decisions we make when it's hard to do the right thing glorify God. And really, we can rejoice in these opportunities because anyone can do the right thing when it's easy. Truly, what we do in the difficult moments is what separates dreamers and doers. The people who live a beautiful, intentional life didn't just have it easy. They made choices when it was hard, and it built their character and refined them.

I wish I could always remember this truth, but sometimes I think about disciplines all wrong. I was tracking my food trying to figure out if what I was eating was causing the heart flutters I had been experiencing and thought to myself, "I don't feel like tracking today. Nobody is telling me to do it so I'm going to stop." This made me smile that I was my own boss and not bound by a journal and pen. I enjoyed about two seconds of freedom with this sentence. It seemed so liberating in the moment. But what freedom is there in not learning what may be causing health issues? What freedom is there in continuing to be distracted by nagging fears?

Hebrews 12:11 has been my go-to verse in helping me stay steadfast in creating new habits and disciplines that I know will glorify God and produce fruit in my life. "No discipline seems pleasant at the time, but painful. Later on, however, it produces a harvest of righteousness and peace for those who have been trained by it." When I remember the fruit that awaits me, I can persevere. When I remember that gratification is delayed and almost never immediate with so many things worth having or doing, I can keep going.

H O M E W O R K

WORK IT OUT

Grab your *Lessons from The Finishing School* workbook
or your worksheet, A GUIDE TO HABITS,
from the website and let the refining begin!

RECOMMENDED RESOURCES

THE COMPOUND EFFECT
book by darren hardy

Find links to the worksheet and extra resources at
VALMARIEPAPER. COM / HOMEWORK.
password: fairlady

8

Blood is Thicker than Paper

A GUIDE TO BOUNDARIES

I had to draw some tough lines in the sand recently when it came to boundaries. It wasn't easy to do, but goodness has it made life sweeter. It started when I suggested to my sister that she should write a devotional for singles. Natalie had been sharing so many things she had learned during a great season of growth and about things she wished other single girls knew. From there, she ran with the idea and created some amazing content for singles. We thought about how fun it would be to work on this project together. How perfect was it that I could design and sell the journal in my shop?

A little backstory. The last few years have not been the easiest in our relationship. Our fighting had reached an all-time high while I was pregnant, and the thought of bringing Vivi into a world where mommy and nanny didn't speak much was enough to send us to see a counselor. We had one impactful session and tons of walls came down. We were able to understand each other so much better, and our relationship flourished like it never had before.

So back to those journals. We launched Natalie's journal in my shop. Things weren't perfect, but we were working on figuring out how the money thing would go. What about sending free journals? Or damaged copies? Who'd pay for the miscellaneous random expenses that would come up? It was a mess. Every conversation we had for a solid few weeks was almost solely devoted to figuring out these logistics. And y'all, we talk like five times a day.

Knowing what an amazing place our relationship had come to, we made a tough decision to keep our businesses separate for the sake of our friendship. Yep, our friendship.

A business coach might have probably said the logical or business savvy approach would be to keep it in my shop, but setting the right personal boundaries aren't always logical to the outside world. Boundaries are beautiful, though. Richard Swenson says, "Boundaries are about establishing a perimeter around the personal and private spaces of our lives and not letting the world come crashing in uninvited. This is not an issue of selfishness but of self-care."

I think we have been victims for too long to a busy life. Here are 4 things that can attribute to our lack of boundaries:

1. We falsely blame people and circumstances for why we are tense, stressed, and unhappy. The truth is, we allowed it to crash in. We give too much power to the person asking of us and not enough power to the fact that WE were the ones who chose to say yes. Instead of using energy to get mad at the person who "made you do it," use that energy to do your best to finish the commitment strong and create a firm boundary for the future.

2. We misinterpret generosity. The Lord desires us to be generous with our time and resources, that is no question. We must use discernment, though. Follow the Lord's leading here instead of giving a blanket yes to every good cause. God gives us all different talents, resources, and passions for a reason. When we say no to the wrong things, we allow for the person who is a right fit to say yes.

3. We want people to like us. Our fragile hearts want to be heroes and rescue the day. We want people to appreciate us. Appropriate boundaries can't happen if that is our ruler by which we gauge each decision. It's time to check our people-pleaser badges at the door and take an oath to stop glorifying this manic state. Yes, you achieved some pretty noble things, but you did so frazzled and frustrated and were impatient with your family in the process. The end doesn't justify the means.

4. We don't value our time. If we did, we would see that maybe God had something bigger planned for that time. It's as simple as that.

This stuff is hard to talk about because we'd all rather be a person who can do it all, but I love not doing it all. I love my life. It's a pretty simple one and maybe even boring to some, and I think a big part of making sure it stays simple is reevaluating things and keeping well-defined boundaries. We can relish in the things we choose not to do just as much as the things we choose to do because we know that when we say no to one thing, we are saying yes to something else. Lin Yutang said it this way, "Besides the noble art of getting things done, there is the noble art of leaving things undone. The wisdom of life consists of the elimination of nonessentials."

Isn't that beautiful? I want to look at a list of things I am not going to do and not feel regret or guilt. I want to see each thing I say no to as white space that will be filled with something good that I may have no idea of right now. I want to feel peace in knowing that it has a purpose.

Last year I was reading a book that everyone had raved about that I just couldn't get into. I read almost the entire book pretty begrudgingly, and then with about twenty pages left, I just put it down and got rid of it. It was so freeing!

Have you ever said no to a project or event that you dreaded the thought of or maybe didn't have an easiness about pursuing? Maybe it was a client who just seemed a little too needy for the services you offered or a project with an organization you weren't really passionate about. I feel pretty empowered when I say no to the things I shouldn't do, but I must make sure I am actually saying yes to the things I want to do. It reminds me that I have some control over what I do and don't do and my actions aren't just left to every single person who drops a request in my inbox. These opportunities beget discernment and discernment begets decision and decision begets courage.

I have had the same experience where I said yes for reasons like the money or the recognition and ended up regretting that decision with every email or phone call about said project. I say I will learn from it the next time, and have mercy, after seven years in business, I'm starting to get it.

Life is a series of seasons. There is a time for planting, for harvesting, and resting. What about the pruning season, when we cut back the branches that have overgrown? An overgrown life (or tree) doesn't produce as much fruit as a healthy, pruned one. It actually weighs it down and breaks the branches. Here I am trying to use my American thinking that more is better or bigger is better. To do the opposite has us up against a world of ads, assumptions, and expectations that make it hard to do anything different. But we must value what God says about pruning over the ideals of the world.

Recently, I said goodbye to designing wedding invitations. As the journals side of Val Marie Paper has grown, the weddings became a smaller and smaller part of our sales. Traditional math would tell me that more streams of revenue make a bigger profit, but it just wasn't adding up for me. When I decided to write a book, I knew I couldn't do everything. Actually, that's not true. Maybe I could have, but it would not have been my best, and I would have been a mess. I would have had a shorter temper with Vivi, been less inclined to serve my husband, and not be the friend I wanted to be.

I looked at my obligations and tried to look at everything both practically and purposefully. This meant I didn't just look at the tangible things like money or time. I looked at what I was most passionate about and what aligned with my purpose. The answer was clear to me. Invitations had to go. This was still not as easy of a decision as it sounds. Sure, I knew it would be smart financially and free up my time, but I have been designing invitations for seven years. It was the thing I have stuck with the longest. I couldn't imagine not doing them. Then one day, I just stopped taking new jobs. It happened without me even noticing really until I sat across the dinner table from my husband and told him I had designed my last one. There was no ceremony, and at this point, I hadn't even mentioned it on social media or my websites.

It all felt very weird, but I was happy to see that pruning had become so natural. As if all those things I had been learning had finally become habit. Lord knows next week I might find myself mixed up in too many activities that results in something out of a hijinx-filled 80s movie (only my favorite movie genre) but for today, I am satisfied with progress and happy to share the tools that have helped me along the way.

One quote that I have written down and carried with me for months is from one of my favorite go-get-em gals, Shelene Bryan. She said, "I'm not afraid most of us will fail, I'm afraid we will succeed at the things that don't matter."

This knocked me on the floor. I am goal-oriented. Accomplishing things comes naturally, but to hear that I could possibly be accomplishing things in areas that don't matter . . . I never even thought of that. I always just assumed that if I was moving forward, I was making progress.

Some examples of this: getting a high score on a computer game or binge-watching *Friends* in a month (guilty!) and less obvious things like winning awards at work but not really living your purpose. Or making enough money to buy all the clothes you want but not helping clothe the poor. If we realize that some of those things we keep saying yes to will help us accomplish things that don't matter, maybe then we will say no because we want to accomplish things that *do* matter.

My advice for doing what matters is to write it out. Clearly define the things you will say yes to and won't say yes to. This can be a filter for all future invitations, opportunities, or commitments.

One very overwhelmed day I found myself making a list of the things I enjoyed doing and the things that stressed me out in hopes of getting rid of those things that stressed me. What I noticed was that some of the items were on both lists. The factor that seemed to determine what side of the list it ended up on was whether my plate was overloaded. When I was able to do each thing well instead of having it be just one more thing to cram in the clown car I called my schedule, I felt more pleasure doing it and less obligation. That taught me that pruning not only helps me get rid of the things I don't need to do but also protects those good things God wants me to do.

It wouldn't hurt to get in a routine of looking through our obligations a few times a year so we can prune back the things that have gotten a little out of control. What things do you want to fill your time? What things do you not want to fill your time? These aren't to be answered willy-nilly but should be based on your priorities in life and God's plan for you. What areas in your life are out of control because you bought the all-too-enticing lie that "you should be doing this," "all good moms DIY," or "all graphic designers offer branding services"?

What things do you need to say no to? What is the cost? And not just the actual cost of time or money but the opportunity cost? Time is your most valuable currency. The number of hours in a day will never change, so I have to stop basing decisions on the assumption that: 1. All will go smoothly, 2. I will be faster, and 3. I'll have help. We have to base decisions on reality. If you are overwhelmed by life right now, there is most likely something you should give up. Evaluate all your current commitments and future commitments with a couple of questions that should help you determine what to say no to:

1. Is this something I am passionate about? Is it part of my core purpose?
2. What obstacles will make this a challenge each week/month/year?
3. What things can I do to streamline or automate this new commitment?
4. Is there a chance that the size of the commitment will change, or am I underestimating the commitment?
5. What does it mean I will miss out on?
6. Is this something God wants me to be a part of? Hopefully, asking the first five questions will help this answer become clear.

Answering these things immediately, before we even commit, will help give us an accurate gauge for how something will alter our daily life balance. You won't be blindsided when a big commitment you've taken on coincides with a big project for work (this is, of course, unavoidable sometimes) and will help avoid those "what did I get myself into?" seasons of life.

Praying about even little decisions is always important. We are inviting God into our decision-making process. You most likely won't get an audible or even clear yes or no, but you can ask God to close doors that need to be closed and open the right ones. You can pray for peace when you make the decision He is calling you to or pray He would stir your heart if you have made the wrong decision. Just remember, boundaries are for your benefit and worth fighting for.

HOMEWORK

WORK IT OUT

Grab your *Lessons from The Finishing School* workbook
or your worksheet, A GUIDE TO BOUNDARIES,
from the website and let the refining begin!

RECOMMENDED RESOURCES

BOUNDARIES
book by henry cloud & john townsend

Find links to the worksheet and extra resources at
VALMARIEPAPER . COM / HOMEWORK .
password: fairlady

9

Spontaneity Loves Structure

A GUIDE TO BALANCE

Right before we bought our first house and moved, I was overwhelmed with chaos. All I wanted was structure because all I wanted was to be spontaneous.

You see, spontaneity loves structure. They seem like the perfect enemies, but without structure, true spontaneity isn't sustainable. Think about that for a minute. Spontaneity needs structure to survive and thrive. I think sometimes we assume that lack of structure is freeing and beautiful, but many times we can feel shackled by the chaos. And that creates absolutely no balance in our life.

The chaos we were living the summer we moved wasn't fun or free. It actually felt like a prison of the unknown, and we just kind of had to be ready for anything. With a little bit of consistency, we make room for fun and more importantly, we make room to say yes to God and the plans He has for us.

This is your guide to creating structure with the intended purpose to help you escape the chaos and live life in the margins. It's a beautiful song and dance between structure and spontaneity that creates balance in our life. I know the word balance can throw up all sorts of red flags for some. We have been taught that it is impossible, and maybe at its core meaning it is. Will the scales ever be perfectly even with spontaneity on one side and structure on the other? Probably not. But I do believe it's possible and beneficial to fall somewhere in the middle of these two extremes.

I have a deep longing to live a life that is free and spontaneous. I want Saturdays to be filled with adventure and to have the flexibility to leave the house at a moment's notice if a friend or family member needs something. I want to give generously if the Lord places it on my heart to do so. Where does the structure come in? If I used my time wisely during my workday, I could be free to have impromptu hangouts with friends. If I fit chores into my weekly schedule, I don't have to skip the Saturday fun and clean all day instead.

So how did I get this ball rolling in my own life? To start, I had to be patient. Structure or creating new routines wasn't going to happen that week we were moving and getting utilities on, walls painted, and boxes packed. There was a lot of pizza and fast food, but that's okay. Structure and a new normal were on the horizon.

Let's look at all the aspects of our lives and how routines can work FOR us. If it happens on a regular basis, it probably needs a routine or a system. Your routines and how you take care of your home, belongings, or car matter for more than just "mommy's sanity" (which is the case in our house many days). Proverbs 27:23 says, "Be sure you know the condition of your flocks, give careful attention to your herds." If you don't have a flock, you aren't off the hook. This passage is basically saying that we should be good stewards of all the things God has entrusted to our care. Don't misuse it like you can pick up another one at Sheep 'R' Us. We have to take care of what God has generously given.

Here are a handful of areas that could benefit from a routine:

Finances
Housekeeping

Grooming
Kids
Fitness
Work Schedule
Church
Home Maintenance
Morning time
Evening time

As you look at your list and the different areas, some will be obvious. You take out the trash every Thursday night. This one in our house gets forgotten so much, though! It seems silly, but it's now on our calendar on the fridge. When we get things out of our brain and onto paper, we can free up the noise in our head—the same kind of noise that distracts us from hearing the Lord. May I never miss something the Lord was trying to prompt me to do over something as menial as taking out the trash.

Others may be less obvious and take some time to research and refine like making time for a weekly or monthly beauty night where you exfoliate, polish, moisturize, or even just making sure you take a vitamin every day.

What about all those little random things that you always forget when you did last? Changed the water or air filter, had the bug guy come by, or changed the batteries in the smoke detector. You could have a home maintenance log with these types of things.

Not every single thing needs to be on paper, but I hope this gives you an idea or jogs your memory on those things that have caused stress or chaos in your life. I, for one, have spent so much time thinking about "Do we need to change the air filter? When did we change it last? Has it already been two months? Maybe we will get to it next month? Is that why our bill is so high? Is that why Vivi has had more allergies?" This is the reality. Things that are very small and routine can keep us busy and distract us from actual important things. I use the air filter as an example because I stared at ours for two weeks on our kitchen counter. I moved it approximately 412 times (give or take a few) and thought about it another 300 times before it was changed. It had way too much of my attention. In the future, I don't want to think about my air filter for more than two minutes every few months.

Now that you have made your list, let's figure out if you have a routine that you are already doing. How will this fit into your schedule? What will it take the place of? If you want to start working out three days a week, it can be really easy to say you will do it. I know for me, I had done that for so long and realized I didn't want to give up my mornings to working out or my evenings with Tyler or my work hours while Vivi was at school. That meant I'd have to choose things that Vivi could do with me. Once I realized this, it became more doable and less of a pipe dream.

I actually have found that kids appreciate a good routine too. Vivi is thriving and finds comfort and security in knowing what comes next. She knows where her clothes go and that she needs to grab a bib when mom starts making food. I am constantly amazed at what she knows and realize it's in part because things follow a pattern, and she has picked up on it. At the same time, it's made her more flexible when we have to switch things up. I honestly don't know the science of why this is, but I like to compare it to music. Do you remember when you were little singing songs with rounds in them? Someone would start singing something, they'd get it down, and then another group would sing something else on top. Without finding our own rhythm before more things were added, it's hard to keep a beat. I got distracted and the melody was lost. But when that first group had time to find a perfect rhythm and that second group was added, it was harmonious and perfect. It sounded better with both parts.

Once you find your beat, it will slowly gain momentum. This is where life hums along and things seem to feel, dare I say, easy. It's when you and your spouse, job, and family life all feel in sync. There are tons of things that can throw you off, even things that are good, but if we have created a routine, it doesn't have to destroy the beat. It can simply add a nice harmony.

It's not rocket science. When life isn't chaotic, we can handle more spontaneity. The example I always think of is how if we don't grocery shop before the week starts or plan our meals, we will eat out more throughout the weekday, usually cheap and unhealthy foods. By Friday when we'd love to go out on a date, we'd blown the food budget and wouldn't really be able to enjoy it because I'd be counting pennies, cutting out appetizers (Tyler's favorite), recommending water for us to drink, or looking for the healthiest item on the menu. So not the caprese or fried jalepenos? Not all of life can be spontaneous, so don't waste your spontaneity on pointless things.

Normally we have a tendency to swing to the extreme of one of these. I tend to swing to the structured side. I even have as one of my prayers in my journal to find a nice balance between structure and spontaneity. I think whichever one we favor can become a stumbling block. We can become too concerned about our structured to-dos and lists to where we are completely blinded to the new mom who desperately needs a pep talk. Or maybe we stay in a chaotic state due to our spontaneity to where we are too busy putting out fires to see what's happening outside our own world.

I've shared tons of tips on how to create structure. Obviously, since that's where I thrive. But what about some tips for those who need to loosen up a bit?

This routine-loving gal is about to discuss "flexibility," so look alive. You might say you don't want to be flexible. The idea of being flexible might make you shudder. But the reality is, if you ARE flexible, it means those things that used to bother you, don't. You aren't resisting being flexible; you are resisting the change.

I prayed all through Vivi's first year and still today that I would be a flexible mom. I don't want to live so rigid that when things are thrown for a loop, my whole world comes crashing down. If Vivi misses a nap when I've got something important to do, I'd prefer the next hour or two to be a pleasant one. If I'm not flexible, it rarely is.

Flexibility is like joy. We have the ability to choose it. And if we don't, we are miserable, so why the heck aren't we choosing it? If you are like me, you might operate off smooth rhythms. This is where you find your groove. To you and me, a change can be like someone throwing a stick in your bike spokes. But if we are willing to accept it, it can instead be like that second harmony that adds a beautiful sound.

As much as I think routines are beneficial, it's my stubbornness to keep things in line that messes me up. Our desire to keep doing things the way we want to do them resists what God wants to do in us. I picture myself putting up my hand and telling God, "No thanks, I'm good." You can't tell, but I'm doing the monkey-with-hand-over-my-mouth emoji. I can't believe I act like that. Each day will not fit the same mold. Can we be okay with that? Can we allow God to rough up our day?

It reminds me of the story in Matthew 19 of the rich young ruler. He asked Jesus what things he needed to do to get eternal life. He knew he was a good rule keeper and had to be a shoe-in. Jesus told him to sell everything he had and give to the poor. He told him his treasure would be in heaven and told the rich young ruler to follow Him. The man declined because he loved his things too much.

God doesn't ask us all to sell everything we own, but if He did would you be willing? If He asked for your home or your Saturday, would you be willing or would life be just a little too chaotic at the moment to say yes?

If spontaneity scares you, be reminded of the hope we have in knowing God is at work. Hope for all the things God has planned for today if you simply unclench your hands and give it to Him. Pray for open eyes to see all God has. I love the word hope, and I love everything I feel when I realize I have it. The possibilities are so great with God. One passage that always moves me is Ephesians 3:20 (MSG). "God can do anything – far more than you could ever imagine or guess or request in your wildest dreams!"

Why does spontaneity love structure?

1. Structure is us being a good steward of our things. Spontaneity is holding it loosely enough for God to do what He wants with it.

2. Structure is proactive to following God's plan instead of being lazy. Spontaneity is reactive to hearing Him speak instead of being too busy doing to hear Him.

3. Structure is details. Spontaneity is big picture.

4. Structure is spending wisely. Spontaneity is having it available for God to use.

So did this chapter make you want to swing in the opposite direction from where you started? God has a purpose for both structure and spontaneity. A life with no spontaneity is rigid, robotic, and unfulfilling. A life with no structure is chaotic, haphazard, and unfulfilling. If we can make both a part of our life, we have the time and opportunity that our structure created and the willing heart and flexibility that our spontaneity created. See there. Spontaneity really does love structure.

HOMEWORK

WORK IT OUT

Grab your *Lessons from The Finishing School* workbook
or your worksheet, A GUIDE TO BALANCE,
from the website and let the refining begin!

RECOMMENDED RESOURCES

MARGIN
book by richard swenson

Find links to the worksheet and extra resources at
VALMARIEPAPER. COM/HOMEWORK.
password: fairlady

10

Not a Tchotchke in Sight

A GUIDE TO MINIMALISM

If there is anything that multiple moves and an up-close look at a hoarded house has taught me, it's that I don't want a lot of stuff. This sounds a lot more noble than it is. The fact of the matter is, I can love the "stuff" just as much as the next person. Seeing a package from Amazon dropped off at my door puts a little spring in my step even if it is just boring old packaging supplies.

But I've had the pleasure of experiencing a minimalist lifestyle out of pure necessity and will never look back. I've already shared on my blog about Tyler's and my journey to owning a home. It started even before that. I went to college a few hours from home and had the extreme pleasure of living in the dorms. This meant each year I'd pack up my stuff, head to school for the year, and then pack it all up to spend the summer at home. That was a total of six moves. Each move, I would go through my things because I was the definition of lazy and didn't want to haul anything I didn't absolutely need. This was the start of my love for decluttering.

So here we are now, in a 1,660ish square-foot house. Let's just say walking the length of this whole place was pretty exhausting initially after living in an apartment that could be vacuumed entirely without moving the cord. The storage is so great that we still have tons of empty drawers and cabinets. We feel like we basically live in *Downton Abbey*. A master bathroom just for me and Tyler? How sophisticated! You mean we don't have to put Vivi's changing table in the dining room? I never imagined it could be so glamorous!

We are living large, y'all. It seems crazy to me that one day there is a very real chance, maybe 90 percent according to what we've heard from others, that our sprawling abbey will soon feel like the guest house. I seriously can't imagine that, *but* we hear it all the time. The house felt huge when they moved in, but slowly shrunk over time and they had to move because they simply needed more space. Houses seem to shrink more than jeans do these days. These stories have resonated with me so much as we moved. Mainly because I'm a little nutty and get hyper aware of possible problems. Because of all this, I was determined not to fill up our home too fast. We had been good at practicing a minimalist lifestyle in our small spaces, but what would happen if we had the space for stuff?

Let's first be reminded of the actual benefits to having less stuff:

1. Less money spent on having to replace or fix items as they break. My mom always told the story her grandpa told her about the real cost when you buy something. His example was a vacuum cleaner. You have to think about what it might cost to get replaced or repaired (this was back when you couldn't run to Target for a cheap replacement). Once you own something, it's unlikely when it breaks you will think "oh we don't need a new one." You will, because you have gotten used to having it. Think about the china or dishes themed for every holiday? Or the corner of the room that just looks naked without "something"? Is it really beneficial or has it become a burden?

2. Less to move. Lazy Valerie here talking. Have you ever filled boxes and boxes and looked around and felt like you didn't make a dent? I am always amazed by the amount of stuff that seems to come out when we actually move. Somehow I've convinced myself that we've got a box for dishes and glassware and one box for appliances and that's it for the kitchen. Six boxes later, and I'm thinking we are definitely going to need more boxes for the rest of the house.

3. Less money spent on a bigger house or storage unit. Tiny homes are all the rage these days for a reason. As the Dave Ramsey generation tries their darnedest to go all gazelle-like on paying off their homes, smaller mortgages are a lot more appealing. And what about these storage units packed to capacity with stuff? There are some very legitimate reasons to have one, but I think the majority of units are simply filled with things we will never in a million years need again.

4. Less time spent picking up or cleaning. This is a big one in the Woerner house. I love having everything tidy, and it is most of the time—something my mother probably never expected from teenage Valerie. Vivi's toys don't overrun the living room, so cleanup is a snap. I feel like more than anything, sometimes cleanup doesn't happen for most people because it feels so overwhelming to tackle. Her small toy messes are always manageable. The laundry, on the other hand…I just conquered Mount Laundry yesterday after two weeks of just admiring the view. That we keep locked away in the laundry room so the rest of the house does feel pretty manageable.

5. Buying fewer things means buying better quality things. I think this is one thing that really appeals to us when we think of minimalism: fewer things, but nicer. I don't think this is the main idea for going minimal, but it is a nice perk. Our *quality* of spending on items is only possible if we can learn to control our *quantity* of spending. And typically, better-quality items should last longer, meaning less shopping, which may mean less spending on extra things that catch your eye, and it pretty much snowballs from there.

This idea doesn't change our mind-set overnight. Chew on this for a while. The more we remind ourselves of these things, the more it becomes a part of our decision-making process. When you get the *envie* (Cajun word for desire or hankering) to go pick up that nearly brand-new furniture piece that you don't need but saw sitting on the side of the road, I hope you will weigh the real cost. A free piece of furniture that never gets used but takes up space and gets moved or scooted around because there is still no proper place for it still costs something.

––––––––––

One of our big "whys" for living minimally was simply our sanity. Unfortunately for us, having a business in our home and just a few feet away at any given moment can make life feel a little cluttered. There are journals and labels and mailers and krinkle. There's paper and plastic and pencils and pens. I can't tell you how much I love taking out the trash every Wednesday after we ship packages. I love getting rid of things. A clutter-free space to me translates to a clutter-free mind. I get so bogged down and almost paralyzed by lots of things. This idea alone helps me reduce the stuff.

But what if you don't feel bothered by the stuff? I would still challenge you to clear out one area, like a closet or even start smaller with a drawer and see if it makes a difference. I think we get desensitized to how stuff can affect us, so you may not even realize how free you *could* feel. It is very much a progression, the same way we don't notice those drawers becoming fuller and fuller until they won't close anymore. The chaos becomes normal, and we don't realize how much it held us back until it's gone.

Now there is nothing in the Bible that says don't buy tchotchkes, but I have found some verses and truths to cling to. This helps me define my "why," and I hope it helps you as well.

Proverbs 24:3-4 (NASB) says, "By wisdom a house is built, and by understanding it is established; And by knowledge the rooms are filled with all precious and pleasant riches."

This verse inspires me to think before filling rooms. It's common sense, but how else do rooms fill up? Do we consciously think, "I want so many things in here that it begins to overwhelm me"? This is never our intent. When we find the perfect "insert whatever you are in the market for at the moment," we don't think twice about how it will fit in the grand picture. We just know we need it. And y'all, this house in Proverbs is filled with precious and pleasant riches. I don't think this means just expensive stuff. I think it means meaningful stuff.

During our own house planning, I had William Morris's quote front and center: "Have nothing in your house that you do not know to be useful, or believe to be beautiful." I took it a step further, though. I wanted things that were mostly useful *and* beautiful. If you had to go through your house right now and name if something was beautiful, useful, or beautiful *and* useful, what would you find? If the answer is "more than you need," here are a few practical and somewhat random tips that have helped us stay tchotchke-free:

1. Do not fill up every cabinet, drawer, or shelf just because "this space needs something." This is so easy to do. We want our home to feel complete and cozy. Our home looks unfinished to some for sure, but we get compliments all the time in how home-y it feels even though 70 percent of our walls are white and unadorned. I really think this is simply because people feel a peace here because of the space to breathe. My gut reaction was to fill every shelf with something decorative, but I could hear the cues from my friends—"need a bigger house," "too much stuff," "outgrew it"—swirling in my head.

2. Everything in its place. When stuff doesn't have a place, it's always moved around. You could move something five times and it's still out because you don't know what to do with it. These objects are the bane of my existence. Sometimes I'll take ten minutes to tidy up, and I'll say to myself, "Everything in its place." This is so motivating to me to figure out a home for those things that just keep floating around instead of continuing the "I'll put it here for now" two-step.

3. Be realistic about what you will actually use or repair. I don't like to DIY. There, I said it. Don't hate me. I just never took to it. I don't think it's fun to hang out in the garage, gather my paint supplies, lay out the newspaper, paint a coat, and then wait. Or worse, have to sand. I don't know if it's my impatience or what, but I will never be the one who will turn an old furniture piece into a work of art. God bless the people who have this talent and better yet, enjoy the process. That is a winning combination right there. Save money and enjoy it? If this is you, keep on collecting pieces, but if you never get around to projects, start saying no. A broken pot that you thought you'd glue back together one day has no value sitting in your garage. I don't mean that in a wasteful way. We need to take care of our things. But don't bring home every donation or free furniture piece.

4. Don't take stuff people offer just because it's free. This is hard, but it goes back to what we talked about in our why. Consider the true cost. Free is hard to pass up sometimes. The allure is more than some of us handle. Why would you turn down something that is free? Because normally it isn't. It will cost time, energy, or actual money for related items or parts. If you wouldn't pay money for it, you probably don't need it.

5. Limit birthday party guests or say no gifts and only buy two or three presents for Christmas and birthdays. Things can get crazy fast in the toy department when birthdays and Christmas roll around. This rule has made things much less overwhelming. For Vivi's first birthday party, we had an intimate party with just family and she got several toys but nothing out of control. For her first Christmas, we got her one gift, a mobile . . . that arrived a few days after Christmas. For her second Christmas, we knew she'd get plenty from the grandparents, so we went practical and filled her stocking with puff snacks. She loved it. She felt like it was Christmas or something. We are trying to set that Christmas bar real low, and I think years one and two were quite a success.

6. Put on your calendar a declutter day or week every quarter. This might sound too often, but it just means it will take less time instead of an eight-hour day in the closet. I have been there, done that, bought the t-shirt, gave it to Goodwill. Follow the seasons. We boxed up some of Vivi's toys and clothes right before Christmas because we knew she'd be getting some new things.

5. Redefine "sentimental" pieces. We can be a sentimental bunch. Many of us are terrified to get rid of things that have been passed down to us. Everything seems sacred. Here's the truth: it's not. Keep a few things that really matter to you, but don't keep everything. It will end up in storage units passed over for generations. And what good did those boxes do for anyone's memories? It's the difference between keeping that old clock that always reminds you of summers on the farm with your grandparents and keeping that old clock that just happened to be in their guest bedroom. My mom is not sentimental and practical to her core. She has already made it clear we can bury her in a shoebox if need be. We aren't going that far, but she has taught me not to place so much value on things. My grandmother died when my mom was just three years old. She doesn't have a ton of things from her but does have a suitcase of old clothes. This is my favorite. She was a mom to three kids in the '60s. When I see the clothes (many of which she made), I can always vividly picture what life was like for her and how she must have been. These have meant more to me than a closet full of odds and ends.

This whole chapter can be boiled down to one idea: Let your home work *for* you, not against you. Our piles that stress us out, the toys we trip over in the dark, the items we can't find when we need them all do us a disservice. The hard pill to swallow is, we caused it. The good news is, we can change it.

HOMEWORK

WORK IT OUT

Grab your *Lessons from The Finishing School* workbook
or your worksheet, A GUIDE TO MINIMALISM,
from the website and let the refining begin!

RECOMMENDED RESOURCES

MARGIN
book by richard swenson

SATISFIED
book by jeff manion

Find links to the worksheet and extra resources at
VALMARIEPAPER. COM/HOMEWORK.
password: fairlady

Brunettes and Civics

A GUIDE TO FRIENDSHIP

I don't remember when it happened or if it's always been this way, but I have trouble making friends. Not in a "nerd in the class" way, just in a "friendship doesn't come naturally" way.

Until recently, I didn't know why, but a light bulb went off during an Influence Network class on Friendships that I haven't been able to turn off.

I have already mentioned that I'm a good girl. I have always been one to follow the rules and color in the lines. People who colored outside of the lines or who used colored pencils instead of crayons scared me. I didn't see how I could be friends with people who didn't think like me. I was worried of judging them or being judged and the possible conflict or awkward conversation that would ensue when we realized we parented differently or believed different things about God. Oh, you thought I was just referring to childhood? Nope.

The truth is, my very best friends growing up (and still today) are very much like me, so from an early age, I saw how "easy" these friendships were. I could completely be myself around them with no thought to if they would judge me. We were all brunettes and talked with the same Southern accent. We drove similar cars and all made good grades. We liked similar music and similar boys (!) so conversations flowed so easily.

The thing was, there were others girls around whom we could have developed friendships with, but they were a little bit different from us. So we didn't. We kept a tight perimeter during youth group activities and just played amongst ourselves. We weren't trying to be mean. We were just young and selfish. I still remember the first time someone told me, "When I first met you, I thought you were so mean. You never talked to me." Ouch. Not the most fun thing to hear, but unfortunately true.

I am now in my thirties and would love to think that I have fully grown out of such high school behavior, but I am just now realizing that I haven't. This idea that I should only be friends with people who are like me because it's easy still influences my thoughts.

Nearly every single one of my good friends has moved away over the last few years, and I have found myself praying every month for new friendships to blossom. I thought this prayer had been mostly unanswered with the exception of a few friends (that I'm not allowing to move away), but now I'm starting to think God probably gave me opportunities that I turned down because I was waiting for the brunette girl with a Southern accent and a Civic.

It reminds me of a funny analogy that is classic in church circles.

A fellow was stuck on his rooftop in a flood. He was praying to God for help.

Soon a man in a rowboat came by, and the fellow shouted to the man on the roof, "Jump in, I can save you."

The stranded fellow shouted back, "No, it's okay, I'm praying to God and he is going to save me."

So the rowboat went on.

Then a motorboat came by. The fellow in the motorboat shouted, "Jump in, I can save you."

The stranded man said, "No thanks, I'm praying to God and he is going to save me. I have faith."

So the motorboat went on.

Then a helicopter came by and the pilot shouted down, "Grab this rope and I will lift you to safety."

To this the stranded man again replied, "No thanks, I'm praying to God and he is going to save me. I have faith."

So the helicopter reluctantly flew away.

Soon the water rose above the rooftop and the man drowned. He went to heaven. He finally got his chance to discuss this whole situation with God, at which point he exclaimed, "I had faith in You but You didn't save me, You let me drown. I don't understand why!"

To this God replied, "I sent you a rowboat and a motorboat and a helicopter. What more did you expect?"

Can you think of any friendship opportunities you have missed? I certainly have. Recently though, I felt some walls of vulnerability come down. All of a sudden I wanted to ask real questions, put my heart out there, and be a real friend. I don't think it's any coincidence that I have been studying about grace and forgiveness.

And I don't think it's any coincidence that this was days before the women's retreat at my church. In years past, I had gone with friends and stuck just with them. This year, I found myself striking up conversations with people. Nothing crazy. I wasn't going to be the next Barbara Walters, but I did get out of my shell.

And it was more than just a few changes in my actions. It was a heart change. I no longer saw our differences as reasons that we couldn't be friends. It didn't scare me off or close me up. The judgment was gone, and I saw opportunities for deep, long-lasting friends everywhere I looked.

Ruth from the Bible is such a great picture of loyalty and friendship. After her husband died, she could have gone back to her family and her hometown and remarried. Instead she chose to stay with Naomi, her sad and depressed mother-in-law, in a foreign land. It seems completely selfless what she did, and she left no room for changing her mind down the road when she said these words in Ruth 1, "Do not urge me to leave you or turn back from following you; for where you go, I will go, and where you lodge, I will lodge. Your people shall be my people, and your God, my God. Where you die, I will die, and there I will be buried. Thus may the LORD do to me, and worse, if anything but death parts you and me."

I desire to have that sort of commitment in friendships. I am very much a work in progress, but thankfully the Lord has been revealing some things to me to guide me along the way.

1. Desire to listen more than you desire to speak. We've all done this. You barely listen to someone because you are just waiting for your chance to talk. If all you want is to be heard, you aren't making friendships, you are creating a posse or fan club.

2. Make a commitment. Time is an indicator of the things we care most about. You don't need to throw your whole world out of whack and forget about margin to have meaningful friendships. Just don't ditch them every time things get a little busy. This lesson has been a hard one for me. When I go through busy seasons, friendships are the first thing I put on the back burner because they don't seem "vital." Ek! Did I just say that? Like I said, work in progress.

3. Share your junk. Going through hard things is an instant bonding agent. When we share our struggles and tears, when we open up our hearts and let someone into the scary places that we would rather keep hidden, we form a bond. That can't happen when we just share surface things.

4. Ask real, thoughtful questions. If you want to get to know someone beyond their occupation or kids' names, you've got to ask real questions. I have two friends that I LOVE to go to lunch with. We always have the most interesting conversations about real things. When I leave them, I feel so refreshed. I would absolutely love the same to be said about me: that people are refreshed after we spend time together.

5. Give grace. I am reminded of all the grace God gives me and that I require so much grace from my friends as well. They love me in spite of my flaws. Why do I forget to do the same?

6. Share a meal. Good conversation can happen sitting across a table from someone where there is no temptation to cut it short like chatting in the carpool lane or while getting groceries. We rarely give ourselves less than thirty minutes or an hour to eat. That's prime talk time.

7. Love selflessly. I almost didn't include this one because I feel like it's too obvious. But really, do I have this down yet? I wish. I don't think it hurts to remind myself and all of us that friendship built on two selfless people is strong and fruitful. A friendship with one selfish person and one selfless person is lopsided, and a friendship with two selfish people has no roots. If we jump ship whenever things get inconvenient or uncomfortable, we should stop pretending we are friends when really we are just hopping on a bandwagon whenever it works for us.

One passage in Scripture that always humbles me is the friendship of David and Jonathan. The words used to describe them would surely make some grown men and even women uncomfortable today, but I love how unabashed and real their friendship was. We could explain away some of their affection and justify that it was a different time and we just aren't like that anymore, but there is one other fact that has me believing this friendship is worth inspiring my own relationships. Jonathan loved so loyally this person who would become king instead of him after his own father. Jonathan becomes friends, closer than a brother, with the one person who will have what he should have had—the throne. I can't help but think about those people that have what I want and how my heart would rather be angry or at the very least prefer to keep a distance instead of love. Jonathan chose the better and encourages me still as I learn how to grow friendships.

Now clearly, I am not a lone wolf. I have great friendships. But I am plenty guilty of letting them stay a bit surface-y or being a person who is hard to get to know. I don't dig into their life or commit like a true friend would. I can laugh and have a good time, but the roots don't run deep. I have had such a longing for deep community. I want to talk about things beyond the weather and Vivi. I want to talk about my heart, and I want to hear from someone else's heart too. So what is it about being known that is so scary?

Donald Miller's book *Scary Close* gave me some great insight.

He talks about how we often try to appear better than we are because we think it will attract others. We don't allow people to know the real us but instead a story we want to tell about ourselves. You know the phrase "reality is better than fiction"? Miller says, "Sometimes the story we're telling the world isn't half as endearing as the one that lives inside us." He goes on to say, "We don't think of our flaws as the glue that binds us to the people we love, but they are. Grace only sticks to our imperfections. Those who can't accept their imperfections can't accept grace either."

Let me tell y'all, I am a sensitive girl, but when we start talking all "you have to love yourself before you can love someone else" type of things, I become like some twenty-something boy who just doesn't get it. And quite frankly, I tend to think it's a load of malarky. But the way Miller puts it makes sense to me.

If we can't acknowledge our own imperfections and accept the grace God has given us, we think we have to look perfect. This is how we keep people at arm's length.

Let me ask you a question. Do your friends know your most embarrassing story? I'm not talking about the one you tell everyone when it comes up at a party. I'm talking about the real embarrassing story. I had both. The one I told people when I was trying to "write my own story," as Donald would say, was of a time we were walking through a creek in the Smokies. I was being a real dare devil and venturing into the middle of the water on rocks. My own story needed to involve me being adventurous because I wanted to impress the boys. Well, I slipped because the rocks were wet, not because I was clumsy, of course. I was drenched in ice-cold water and blinded by the splashing. I tried to get out of the water and lunged out and slammed my head into a tree. And a group of four maybe five perfect strangers saw it. How humiliating! It really wasn't, but it did provide the perfect story to prove I was adventurous, outdoorsy, and tough—all things I was not.

My real embarrassing story happened during a little league game. My sister and I were easily the worst on the team, the subs. I had to go to the bathroom, but if you left the dugout, you couldn't play. I didn't want to miss my two innings to play, so I held it. Then I batted and actually got on base! I'm sure they walked me. I was shorter than most, and that was my saving grace for getting on base. I was on second and just couldn't hold it any longer. I peed right there standing on second base. Yep. You heard right. When we reached the dugout, I started splashing water on my legs because I was so "hot and sweaty" and quietly prayed that this was something athletes did. The girl who was on first base came to me and said, "Did you just pee on second base?" With a swagger of a born athlete, I lied and said, "No. I'm just really hot and sweaty."

How often do we pick and choose what story to tell based on how it will make people see us? Why do I think people want perfection out of their friends? I know that's not what I look for in friends. I want real people in my life. I want to be friends with the kid who peed on second base, not the girl who shared a story that is so lame and not embarrassing that I'm afraid to be myself and share my real story. Instead of a bracelet or blood, can we seal a friendship pact by sharing our deepest, darkest secrets or embarrassing stories and loving each other anyway?

I've been making baby steps as I learn what it means to be a friend. One day, after days of having all three of us in our little family sick, I had a text message from a friend I was supposed to have a play date with soon. She asked if she could help. My immediate mental response was, "No, we are great!" This statement made a liar of me, though. I had just cried my eyes out in the car for twenty minutes because I was exhausted and needing help.

I told her, "Thanks! Normally I won't let anyone help besides my sister or mom, but I'm working on that. I'll probably text you today or tomorrow!" She completely understood what I meant. It's amazing how much we can relate to others when we are honest. Not three hours later I texted back to say I could really use someone to drop off a few packages at the Post Office. And she said yes. Why are we so afraid to let people help us? Especially when they are willing? Is it because we think they are just being polite? Maybe that's true sometimes, but give them the benefit of the doubt. And loosen up about it. One day your friend or that person you want to be friends with will need a favor back, and you will gladly say, "I can do that for you!"

To initiate a friendship or to take one deeper requires vulnerability and the willingness to get hurt. They don't just fall into our laps. They take work and time and honesty. We may get embarrassed or crushed in the process, but that's not the end of the story, and it shouldn't be a reason not to try. Friendships are a sweet spot in life. They make good news even more of a celebration, and they make bad news not hurt so much. Ecclesiastes 4:9-10 (ESV) says, "Two are better than one, because they have a good reward for their toil. For if they fall, one will lift up his fellow. But woe to him who is alone when he falls and has not another to lift him up!"

H O M E W O R K

WORK IT OUT

Grab your *Lessons from The Finishing School* workbook
or your worksheet, A GUIDE TO FRIENDSHIP,
from the website and let the refining begin!

RECOMMENDED RESOURCES

SCARY CLOSE
book by donald miller

Find links to the worksheet and extra resources at
VALMARIEPAPER. COM/HOMEWORK.
password: fairlady

12

Stupid Ice Cream

A   G U I D E   T O   H O S P I T A L I T Y

We've lived in our fair share of tiny places that always made entertaining a little difficult. Not having a dining room table for two years will definitely put a damper on inviting friends over for dinner. When we moved, I was itching to host our friends in our new home. As a former wedding planner who had just hung up her headset, nothing sounded better than getting to create invitations and come up with themes for parties.

What I wasn't counting on was how different hosting in our home was compared to planning weddings. My job had been to make things happen behind the scenes. We literally wore black for the sole purpose of blending in and not being noticed. I was so accustomed to keeping my head down, getting the work done, and doing it all with a smile. Now I was expected to make more than the quick wedding guest chat? I was expected to listen well and ask thought-provoking questions?

As it turns out, I am not a great hostess by trade, though the wedding planning business I owned should have told a different story After six months, seven parties, and dozens of small groups later, I have learned a few things.

That first lesson came when we hosted my sister's and my

thirtieth birthday party. I had been dreaming all year to be moved into our house (wherever that would be) by the time I turned thirty so I could have a big party. And would you believe it, it actually worked out the way I had envisioned. This being our first big party at the new house, I thought I'd be extra fancy and create a menu that was, well, not a smorgasbord. Tyler had been getting into making his own pizza sauce and crust, so interesting pizzas and toppings sounded perfect. I started thinking about what to pair with it and thought only Italian foods would do. We couldn't go mingling our food ethnicities. At least not at my fancy party. So for apps we had garlic bread with a trio of sauces, alfredo, marinara, and I forget the third. Coincidentally, so did everyone at the party. I'm pretty sure we had more sauce at the end of the party than before guest arrived. You figure that one out. The pizza was gobbled up and enjoyed, but I wanted guests to love everything. I learned a life lesson in that sauce. Give the people their dang meatballs and hummus, and they will come.

As I mentioned, this was our thirtieth birthday party, and my body did not let me forget it. I had a headache the whole time, but refused to take medicine because I hate taking medicine and like to think I'll just get over it, but I ruined my good time and I was *not* a good-time gal. And I mean that in the clean old lady cliché way, I'm guessing not however urban dictionary would define it. A good-time gal has fun and is fun. Instead, I sat on the couch half-listening and sort of laughing at what I could hear over my pounding headache and my own thoughts about how old this made me feel. If you every feel sick or icky before a party, by all means make an exception to your medicine rule. Everyone will love you for it and be chanting, "Good-time gal, good-time gal!" with you on their shoulders.

One of my very favorite parties was actually one my sister planned. I use this term loosely, because really she just invited everyone to our house for Halloween night in a group text the day before. And everyone was up for it. We put on a pot of chili, and people brought chips and drinks and can I tell y'all? It was simply the best. I don't remember the exact conversations, but I remember laughing and people staying well after that chili was gone. There were babies dressed in costumes. You have not seen cute till you've seen a baby dressed up like a crawfish.

I might have flown too close to the sun and got cocky, because during our super bowl party I got burned. Yes, I did in fact say *during*. The husband was making bowls of ice cream. Me being the brilliant hostess I was, I told him to make sure to use the smaller bowls. I didn't want to run out of ice cream before everyone got some. Tyler is a notorious "big portioner." I also didn't want their average scoop to look like we had served them the equivalent of a shot in a Route 44 Sonic cup. When I came back a few minutes later, pardon my Spanish, it was "no bueno." Tyler ran out of ice cream . . . while he was making my bowl. (Insert emoji crying hysterically here). If you know me well, you know ice cream, especially Blue Bell, is one of my favorite sweets. So this bummed me out, but I also cared way too much about how stupid the ice cream looked in the big bowls. Did you know ice cream could look stupid? I tried so hard to prevent it. Alas, it happened anyway, and this didn't sit well with me.

Again, I wanted to be a good-time gal. But you know who's not a good-time gal? Someone who just had an argument with her husband during a party over ice cream bowls. I don't remember who won the game or what tear-jerking commercials came on. All I remember was quietly stewing over those darn ice cream bowls. He thought all I really cared about was my ice cream and not our guests, and all I cared about was how stupid the ice cream looked, which unfortunately, did not make me any less crazy.

The truth is, it didn't matter how the ice cream looked in the bowl, I had some learning to do. Hospitality is not about me.

Romans 15:7 (ESV) says, "Therefore welcome one another as Christ has welcomed you, for the glory of God." I want to give what is actually needed (a happy un-awkward environment for our guests), not what I think is needed (perfectly portioned ice cream).

This experience got me real intentional about the Galentine's Day Party I was hosting just a few weeks later. I even had it as one of my goals that month to be an intentional and a gracious hostess, and, you know, a good-time gal. Nerding it up as I usually do, I researched articles or tips on how to be a good hostess. I decided any articles written by my girl Shauna Niequist (whom I wish I was best friends with and would attend my next Galentine's Day Party) were my go-to resources. After reading her book *Bread & Wine*, I fell in love with the idea of community and figured she'd be the perfect person to show me how to make it happen.

And there it was. A beacon of truth amidst a sea of social graces and "have music on and a drink ready" and other great but surface-y advice.

"True hospitality is when someone leaves your home feeling better about themselves, not better about you."

Take that in for a minute. I have had it so backwards. We are overly concerned about the food being perfect or the floors being swept. We want to impress our guests, but our guests just want to enjoy our company and feel good about themselves after they leave. And that's what I realized I want my guests to feel, though I had been going about it the wrong way. I thought they'd feel good if they liked me.

Shauna also put it another way in *Bread & Wine*, "Focus on making people comfortable, on creating a space protected from the rush and chaos of daily life, a space full of laughter and safety and soul."

I want people to feel accepted and valued the moment they arrive at my house. To be able to provide that for someone seems so special as I focus on serving their needs above my own.

How do I make that happen? We have to listen. I think in our "me, me, me" world, it is so easy to talk and need to be heard and half listen as we wait for someone to take a breath so we can speak. It is such a heart issue, this whole being hospitable thing. When I start from the inside and decide all my decisions will be based on how I want others to feel when they are in our home, I think the rest will follow nicely.

An article by Zoe Nathan in *Darling Magazine* said it this way: "The perfectly imperfect hostess knows that it's more important everyone finds his or her own happy place at the party rather than everything tasting amazing."

Acts 28:2 illustrates this by saying, "The islanders showed us unusual kindness. They built a fire and welcomed us all because it was raining and cold." A fire for my damp and cold body would be my happy place indeed!

There are three characteristics that I see are needed for us to show hospitality well:

1. Listen tentatively - So we can actually hear the needs, even the ones they aren't speaking.

2. Love unconditionally - So others are free to be themselves completely.

3. Serve joyfully - So others feel comfortable accepting your hospitality.

What does hospitality look like for me? I know I've mentioned parties, but there are so many other ways I want to show hospitality and grow our community.

I want more dinners around the table. I want traditions and

memories that mean something for our family. Traditions or routines that show Vivi and future Woerner babies a consistency and provide a happy place for them. I want to invite more friends over for intimate dinners sitting outside under the bistro lights as we listen to the frogs and try not to get eaten up by mosquitoes.

I want to visit my grandma more, to hear her stories of my grandpa and to see her face light up when Vivi gives her hugs and kisses. I want lunches with friends that feed my soul and refresh me because the conversations were that real and that good.

What do you want?

I'll close with a quote from Shauna because her words make me want community and I want you to want community too. "This is about a family, a tribe, a little band of people who walk through it all together, up close and in the mess, real time and varnished."

Now that we know what is important, here are a few random tips that are a tad on the surface-y side I hated on earlier that will hopefully make way for community.

1. Be dressed early. Nothing is more stressful than having no makeup on when guests arrive. Nobody can help you apply mascara, but they can help slice bread or open a bottle of wine. So if something is left until the last minute, make it the food and not you.

2. Drink green juice or eat healthy the day of your party. One of the last parties I hosted, I had something super unhealthy for lunch and felt sluggish and sick. I'm showing my age here, but I had to lie on the couch for a little while when I could have been prepping things, which made for a more hectic afternoon.

3. Serve foods that are crowd pleasers. See the aforementioned untouched sauce tale for details.

4. Serve foods that do not need to only be eaten at the perfect temperature. Food is going to sit around for a little while. There is no sense in getting your panties in a twist over crusted over queso dip.

Free idea: I would love if someone would create a website where you can ask guests to fill out a quick survey (like 5 questions) of their favorite apps, drinks, and any dietary restraints. Then for your next party, you could plug in all the guest who RSVP yes and see exactly the ratio of Dr. Pepper and Coke or red and white wine drinkers you have and whether the meat extravaganza dish will go untouched by the room full of pesca-, veggie- and fruiti-arians. If you do create this or if there is one out there already, please email me the link, and I will be the first to sign up.

H O M E W O R K

WORK IT OUT

Grab your *Lessons from The Finishing School* workbook
or your worksheet, A GUIDE TO HOSPITALITY,
from the website and let the refining begin!

RECOMMENDED RESOURCES

BREAD & WINE
book by shauna niequist

Find links to the worksheet and extra resources at
VALMARIEPAPER. COM / HOMEWORK.
password: fairlady

13

Never Been Kissed

A GUIDE TO WAITING

Everyone is waiting on something. If it's not marriage, it's college, a family, a house, having your kids out of the house, retirement, etc. Being in this "in between" where we want to (or have to) leave and where we hope to go is tough.

As a planner, there is nothing I want more than to know what the future holds so I can plan accordingly. Can you even picture the sort of calendar of to-dos we'd make for ourselves if we knew when each milestone would arrive? Trust would be nearly obsolete because who needs trust when we have our well-mapped-out future? With that, I can set my own course to get there. That is the beauty of waiting, friend. It causes us to cling to God because He alone knows the path before us.

Waiting always has a purpose. Deuteronomy 8:2 says, "Remember how the LORD your God led you all the way in the wilderness these forty years, to humble and test you in order to know what was in your heart, whether or not you would keep his commands."

As I write this, we just found out that month four of trying for baby #2 was a no-go. For Baby #1, now known as Vivi Mae or Tootsie, we got a yes that first month. I knew I'd need to keep my expectations in check, but gahhhh-lly. Easier said than done. I didn't realize how much I expected it to be quick until I got that first no. Luckily, through past experiences with waiting, God has taught me a few lessons, and I've been quicker to slow down and pace myself knowing God has not forgotten me. One thought He keeps reiterating to me is that He knows the right season for us to welcome another baby, I don't. And me being the perfectionist I am, I much prefer God's plan to any silly thing I could throw together.

————————

This has been my story of waiting. This is how God taught me His timing is better than mine.

The facts: I went 24 1/2 years without a single boyfriend. Unless you count the boy I dated for 4 days and literally had to break up with him because I had knots in my stomach our entire courtship. And unless you count that boy I dated for a blissful week in sixth grade who had his friend, someone I personally couldn't stand, tell me in line heading out to recess, that his buddy wanted to break up with me. How childish, I thought! This was actually very fitting, though, being the ten-year-olds that we were. I made myself feel better later learning that he did in fact want to date me but his friend didn't want him having a girlfriend. So yay. Ego repaired. I know all this because it was carefully documented in my diary.

But all the other 8700+ days, I spent single. And as for kisses, the first happened at eighteen, and by today's standards it would be considered a handshake. It was a peck and a good six years before a real kiss with my now husband.

Looking back, I don't regret the wait for one day. God gave me a person beyond my wildest dreams. I can't imagine what life would be like had I settled for less than his best.

I don't say that to pat myself on the back. It all started with a prayer I read in Elisabeth Elliot's book *Passion and Purity* that became my prayer early on in high school. She said she prayed the Lord would put her heart (and romantic desires) asleep until it was time for her to meet her mate, much like God put Adam to sleep to create Eve (Genesis 2:20-22).

How excited I was to make that prayer my own! It seemed so safe to protect my heart from heartache! And I believe it did, but the following eight years weren't easy. I definitely had my fair share of crushes—no feelings returned, though, thank you. And a few vice versa.

Off I went to college, thinking *surely* I'll find Mr. Right amidst these 5,000 new boys. Four years later it became, surely I'll meet him when I return home from college and begin my career. I actually did meet Tyler the month I came home, but it took two years for my heart to "wake up" to him and God's perfect timing.

I remember asking God so many times, why does "so and so" have so many boyfriends/opportunities? All I want is ONE! I thought it was a very unselfish thing to just ask for one. It was hard to watch as Valentine's or Christmas rolled around knowing the present on the table or flowers that were delivered were not for me. And of course, the inevitable thought that came in my head was, "What is wrong with me?"

Had I known I'd find Tyler at all, I probably could have been a bit more patient. I think most things in life are like that. It's the unknown that's scary. Why would God suddenly drop the perfect man for me in my lap without giving me any practice runs? Or something to prep me? Ironically, he did prep me. I had enough good guy friends to start a baseball team, and with each one, I learned about relationships with the opposite sex.

One of my favorite things about journaling is going back to read old journals about times I faced different trials and see what is different now or how the Lord answered those prayers. I can't tell you how many times I cried out to God wondering where the heck he was in terms of my relationship status. Did He forget? Surely He couldn't with all my helpful reminders.

The craziest thing is that when I finally did find Tyler, I remember thinking, "That was fast!" What? Had I forgotten the last long eight years? I kind of did, actually. Having Tyler was answer enough. He was worth it. And those years didn't matter anymore. In hindsight, it is always so easy to see God's hand at work. Had I known what God had planned, I'm sure I would have handled things a bit better. But now I have this little story to remind me when I can't see how God could possibly use this situation or that. I think back on how confused and frustrated I was, and I picture God glancing down from heaven just kind of smirking thinking, "I've got something so amazing planned for you, you have no idea!"

I have already said how beautiful the waiting can be. Here are a few specific reasons why:

1. It refines our soul. God has a purpose for waiting even when we can't see it. And most of the time, we won't see it until it's well behind us. Lamentations 3:25-28 (CEV) says, "The Lord is kind to everyone who trusts and obeys him. It is good to wait patiently for the Lord to save us. When we are young, it is good to struggle hard and to sit silently alone if this is what the Lord intends."

2. It demands our honesty. Reading the Psalms and hearing David pour his heart out to God always reminds me of how desperate we are as we wait for God. Other times, we may try to do it on our own, but in this humble position, we have nothing left to lose but to give God our full heart and every honest thought. Rock bottom is not a place to save face. It's a place of bowing our head low and crying out to God.

3. It reminds us that with God, we are more capable

than we know. When I would hear stories of friends going through trials, I always used to think I could never handle it. But then they would feel the same about my trials. Until we go through something, we always feel incapable, but that's because we are just accounting for our own strength and not God's.

I have moments of strength where the process and the waiting excite me because I know I am being refined and clearly remember all those things I just mentioned about how beautiful waiting is. My pastor said once in a sermon: if you respond well, it can be the most fertile season of your life. I want that. But I am inevitably faced with the reminder—maybe a pregnant friend or that mom younger than me who has already had four babies. Waiting can be easy until we add in other people to the equation. They serve as a constant metric to where we think we should be or simply could be.

I have a model example about the waiting in my twin sister, Natalie. She is unmarried at thirty years old, which might as well be a crime here in the South or at the very least worth a barrage of questions as people try to Sherlock Holmes the mystery of why she is still single. Having a sister who is married with a little girl has piled on new ways of torture in the form of "Are you the married one? . . . Or the other one?" That sister of mine never throws a pity party. She has her rough days, of course, but she's secure in God's plan. It's why she wrote singles' devotional this year. It's intended for singles, but I think it helps with so many other seasons of waiting.

She shares ideas that I think all too often we don't want to hear. What happens if that thing we are waiting for never happens? God doesn't promise we will have all the babies we want or the perfect job. In one chapter, Natalie references Luke 16:15b (CEV), "The things that most people think are important are worthless as far as God is concerned." She goes on to say that desiring for marriage or babies or a house or whatever your current waiting season is aren't bad, but it's just not biblical to say that they are our life's goal. And if that's the case, then anything we are waiting for, though important to us, shouldn't become what we fixate our life on. Natalie said, "Until we realize that this is not our goal for our time on earth, we will feel entitled to these things," and that entitlement only makes the wait that much harder.

Ironically, the most important thing—a relationship with God and the invitation to spend eternity in heaven with Him—are things we don't have to wait on. We can have them right now. And although everything else pales in comparison, He graciously walks beside us in the waiting.

HOMEWORK

WORK IT OUT

Grab your *Lessons from The Finishing School* workbook
or your worksheet, A GUIDE TO WAITING,
from the website and let the refining begin!

RECOMMENDED RESOURCES

PASSION & PURITY
book by elisabeth elliot

WHOLEHEARTEDLY
singles' devotional - nataliemetrejean.com

Find links to the worksheet and extra resources at
VALMARIEPAPER.COM/HOMEWORK.
password: fairlady

Harry Potter Does Broadway

A GUIDE TO JOY

I have learned that there are a few keys to having joy: serving others, exercising gratitude, and having a heavenly perspective. We say joy is a choice. If you have trouble choosing joy, choose to do the following three things, and I think joy will come.

SERVE OTHERS

I know for me, when I have experienced unexplained sadness, my analytical side just has to view this thing from all angles in hopes of figuring out a way to experience joy. That means a lot of self-reflection (otherwise known as time spent thinking about ME). I do it all in the name of trying to find joy when, really, if I simply took my focus off myself long enough to serve someone else, the joy would flow.

We all know this. I don't even feel like I need to give you tons of examples of serving to convince you, so I'll keep it short. Look for people to serve and love well. Be vigilant and, if you are the obsessive type, go ahead and be a little obsessed. It's better than being obsessed with yourself.

GRATITUDE

This elusive little booger can drive us insane. We all want to be grateful, but there are a million things that keep us from it, like our "grass is greener" mentality, our "I'll be happy when" mentality, and so much more.

I remember being in New York sitting in a Broadway play thinking about all the adventure the next day would hold. Suddenly reality hit me and I thought, "Your favorite thing about NYC is always the Broadway shows. Why aren't you enjoying it? Why are you looking ahead to tomorrow?" That was a turning point for me about how easily it is to take moments for granted that in the past we hoped for. I don't think I ever appreciated the theater so much. I sat and enjoyed the heck out of Daniel Radcliffe in *How to Succeed in Business without Really Trying*. And this coming from a Muggle. Only Potterheads will get that reference.

It seems I live life like this a lot: always looking forward to the next thing, not even realizing that where I am is where I have been praying, striving, or working to get to. I hate that. I can be so cavalier about the gifts God gives me.

We were getting our home ready for a photo shoot to be featured on a blog recently. I was making sure everything was in its perfect place, and it mostly was. But there was this one roman shade that was messed up, and it taunted me. As I was fiddling with the shade, a thought popped into my head that could have only come from God. "What then?" When the shade is fixed and the house is perfect, when I'm done fussing over our new home, what will I do then?

This "What then?" place had always felt so far away, like it would never happen. We waited, which taught us so much patience, but did we place too much emphasis on the material world instead of focusing on our heavenly perspective? Here I was on the edge of what I considered complete, and God asked, "Are you done? Can we enjoy this place now or are you going to move the line of content?"

A constant state of striving for "more" steals our joy. Joy becomes a place we leave so that we can chase after that same joy that we think is on the horizon. It's right here, though, right in front of me. Ungratefulness reveals an icky part of our thinking.

Ann Voskamp said, "You would be very ashamed if you knew what the experiences you call setbacks, upheavals, pointless disturbances, and tedious annoyances really are. You would realize that your complaints about them are nothing more nor less than blasphemies - though that never occurs to you. Nothing happens to you except by the will of God, and yet [God's] beloved children curse it because they do not know it for what it is."

Can this be said of you? I know it has been true for me way too many times. If you have not read Ann's book, *One Thousand Gifts*, I highly recommend it. It was so impactful to how I saw God's work in my life and one reason why I created the Gratitude Journal. Our days are vastly different the moment we allow gratitude in. And the truth is, we only see it because we are looking. I wrote this note on my phone about four years ago while living in our least ideal condition.

What an amazing and unorthodox way to live?! If I truly find blessings in every day, every day is a good day. I'm laying here after waking up and reading *One Thousand Gifts*. It's changed the way I look at my day and it's literally 2:23 AM in the middle of the night and I can't sleep because I keep thinking how amazing today was. And guess what? Nothing special happened. I worked from home all day. Didn't put on makeup or even real clothes. Tyler got home with pizza for dinner. We ate. Read. Then picked up chai lattes from CCs. Went home to organize my office and here I am. Unable to sleep because of giddiness. What a difference mindset makes!

I want that sheer can't-sleep excitement over a routine day every day. Can you imagine what this world would be like if we lived like that? I can't even explain what my reasoning was to feel the way I did except to say I had a huge appreciation for exactly what was in front of me. Now to a mom that day sounds anything but mundane, but it was to the newlywed. And today's mundane may be tomorrow's bliss. If that's the case, that's all the more reason to appreciate it.

I think our expectations can sink us when it comes to living with joy. It's rooted in pride like all sin. We feel entitled to certain things, and anything less is simply not good enough. When we approach things with humility, whatever is done to us or given to us is seen as a blessing. It changes everything. But I forget so often that humility is a choice. And that joy is a choice too. Can you think of a time when you simply chose to not have joy in your own life? I can. And I hope you don't hate me when I share this.

My life is pretty cush. I am married to a hilarious husband who enjoys cooking every night. I am mom to a sweet toddler who's an absolute peach (most of the time). I get to work from home while she's at school or sleeping. I live four doors down from my parents who drop medicine off at my door late at night or watch Vivi when I need "fifteen minutes." My life isn't hard. I don't say that to brag at all, because some days, I think, "Oh I wish I had just fifteen more minutes to read a book or something!" Really? I wake up three hours before my kid does and have two kid-free hours almost every night. I get "me time." But this can be the reality. There is this sick little hunger in me that constantly wants more. It's our flesh. I can be just as unhappy as someone who doesn't have five minutes to themselves during a day, and that says something.

It really is all about perspective. Oh, you are sick of hearing that one? Take it from me, someone who found myself unhappy even though I had more than enough time to write a book in six weeks. Don't look to anyone else's life or even your own life kicked up a notch and think you will be happy "when." Learn to have joy now. Learn to have joy when it's hard. Then you will know how to have joy when things feel easy too.

HEAVENLY PERSPECTIVE

I have found that when all else fails and the world is just really hard and throwing everything it's got at you, finding even a handful of things to be grateful for is tough. But we always have one gift—in fact it's the greatest gift—that as believers we can rejoice in and never lose. And it just took me the last nine miserable days to appreciate it.

We have spent the last week and a half in the Woerner house with either the flu or cold, multiple double ear infections, an after-hours walk-in clinic visit for two (daddy-daughter style!), a 4 AM ER visit, and a pediatrician visit. I'm recognizing pharmacists at our corner drug store even through the fog of sinus headaches, and the amount we had planned to save this month evaporated the second we walked in the ER. One thing I realized about having everyone in the house sick is that there was no cheerleader. There was no one to find the silver lining. There was no one to stay positive or rally the troops, just three very needy and annoyed people. I think around day four or five with no tip of the thermometer, I started to laugh. I mean, this had to be some joke the Lord was playing on me. I like to think I am a positive person, but this was putting me through the ringer, and I'm just glad I'm not on a reality show because it would have been the most dramatic episode yet.

All right, Lord, I give up. We can cut the chapter on joy! Now can I go three minutes without blowing someone's nose? All this during Easter week. I thought surely Good Friday would be the darkest day. God is symbolic like that sometimes, or at least that's what I expect. But Saturday was hard, and Sunday passed with no fancy dress, no Easter basket for Vivi, and definitely no family photo. Oh, but y'all! Easter day did bring some semblance of joy when reality hit. These things are all temporary. I had been trying to muster up joy around me. I wrote things in my gratitude journal like hot tea or a hot bath. It was true, but I was reaching and wrote it as if someone were forcing me to move my pen and less from the heart. The truth was, to find joy I could look no further than the reality of the cross. I could celebrate the incredible love God has for us and the sacrifice Jesus made for you and me! I could celebrate a God who does exactly what He said He would do. I could celebrate a God who gives way more grace than we ever deserve. And I could celebrate our future home in heaven forever with God that Jesus's death on the cross made way for.

And on top of that, I could celebrate the refining that was happening in me as I faced the trials like James 1:2-4 (ESV) talks about. "Count it all joy, my brothers, when you meet trials of various kinds, for you know that the testing of your faith produces steadfastness. And let steadfastness have its full effect, that you may be perfect and complete, lacking in nothing." In high school, this was my favorite Scripture. I have no idea if I truly understood what it meant other than knowing good things came out of even bad times, but that was enough to rest my joy on.

The Lord has delivered me from pain and suffering that has no end. He's delivered me from life that is apart from Him. If my worst days where I feel far from God are any glimpse into what I have been saved from, I am thankful. This is why we have a joy that never fades. You might feel like this world dealt you a crappy hand, but the truth is, God is going to use it and then He's going to follow it up with eternal life *if* we choose to receive it. If you aren't a believer yet and looking for a sign that this is for you: Hi! This is your sign. He's longing for you so dearly to come to Him and experience His overwhelming joy.

2 Corinthians 4:16-18 says, "Therefore we do not lose heart. Though outwardly we are wasting away, yet inwardly we are being renewed day by day. For our light and momentary troubles are achieving for us an eternal glory that far outweighs them all. So we fix our eyes not on what is seen, but on what is unseen, since what is seen is temporary, but what is unseen is eternal."

Joy comes when we live in light of the reality of heaven. How exciting is it to watch a game you know your team will lose? Even little victories like a good pass or a touchdown seem empty if we know the outcome. But as believers, we know the outcome of this life. We know God reigns, and that is cause for celebration in even the most mundane parts of our day.

Joy is a funny thing. Ann put it best when she said, "Is it only when our lives are emptied that we're surprised by how truly full our lives were? Instead of filling with expectations, the joy-filled expect nothing — and are filled . . . My own wild desire to protect my joy at all costs is the exact force that kills my joy."

Stop looking for joy and start choosing it. Live with gratitude, serve others, and live in light of eternity. There you will find joy.

HOMEWORK

WORK IT OUT

Grab your *Lessons from The Finishing School* workbook
or your worksheet, A GUIDE TO JOY,
from the website and let the refining begin!

RECOMMENDED RESOURCES

ONE THOUSAND GIFTS
book by ann voskamp

MY NAME IS HOPE
book by john mark comer

VMP GRATITUDE JOURNAL
lined journal - valmariepaper.com

Find links to the worksheet and extra resources at
VALMARIEPAPER.COM/HOMEWORK
password: fairlady

15

Easter Sunday Best

A GUIDE TO CONTENTMENT

To live a life content. It sounds so idealistic. How can I possibly reach a point where everything in front of me is all I need? Especially when we are surrounded by things that tell us we just need a little more. We could get everything we want and in that moment, it's somehow still not enough. This has been true for me countless times, but I don't want it to be true for me anymore.

My quest for contentment all started with another quest. One for margin. I realized I wanted less. But what happens when you get rid of the excess and more wants to creep in? What happens when we are no longer content with less? It's a heart matter, and my heart loved stuff. But really, only for about fifteen minutes of a new purchase. Then my heart got annoyed with the stuff.

Am I the only one who thinks that once I get myself organized, which always means new things to help me get organized, that I'll have it together? Example. Once I get that cute expensive purse with dividers, my purse will never be messy again. This keeps me in hot pursuit of that elusive tool that will change everything when in reality, my life would be much more satisfying if I simply changed my mindset.

I desperately want this shift to happen. I want to see an

Anthropologie catalog as inspiration to my creativity, not stuff I need. I can just imagine getting the beautiful new issue in the mail and thumbing through looking at colors and textures and noticing all the amazing details. I could appreciate the artistry and the patterns, even the location. As I flip to the final page, I could feel inspired and refreshed instead of that sudden feeling of "I don't make enough money, I'm not skinny enough to pull that off, or my house will never be that cute."

Ah! The pinnacle of contentment. When I can look at the stuff and not instantly feel the need to buy it, oh that will be a happy day indeed. We know the stuff doesn't matter. We know it doesn't last. We know that it might only take two days before I toss it to the side and forget about it. And we know God is more important. Matthew 6:19-21 (ESV) tells us, "Do not lay up for yourselves treasures on earth, where moth and rust destroy and where thieves break in and steal, but lay up for yourselves treasures in heaven, where neither moth nor rust destroys and where thieves do not break in and steal. For where your treasure is, there your heart will be also."

If this verse was visual in my life, like if my stuff looked like treasure and I saw a bank account of deposits being taken out of heaven every time I "laid up" treasures here on earth, maybe I would get it. I don't see it like that, though. Many times I give absolutely no thought to what I'm doing and simply do it. Proverbs 5:6 says, "She gives no thought to the way of life; her paths wander aimlessly, but she does not know it." My lack of contentment is usually a result of me living aimlessly instead of rooted and grounded. This is evident in the way I shop. I shop for things I THINK I need for a successful business, to help me stay organized, to motivate me to work out, the list goes on. Having a business account means I can look picture perfect to my husband, because I never buy clothes with our personal account. At the end of the year, this miscellaneous category that cannot be written off as a business expense is technically considered my income. This makes me cringe! I would never spend the amount of money I spend on clothes and other items if it were as transparent to my husband as the number I see in this category. Just being honest here.

So I decided to do something about this. A few months ago, I started the Contentment Challenge. I had heard Nancy Ray talk about this for a few years but never attempted on my own because it seemed a little extreme; also, I was pregnant at the time and shopping was going to happen. Here were the rules:

No shopping for three months for anything but necessities. That meant no clothes, no home goods while strolling through Target, etc. Instead putting that energy into enjoying life's little pleasures that God brings rather than things, giving away clothes and reading inspiring books. Several books that reinforced the idea behind the contentment challenge across all spectrums were: *7, The Hole in the Gospel, Margin, 168 Hours* and *Love, Skip, Jump.*

If this idea scares you, if you can't imagine giving up the stuff, you need to do it. Hebrews 13:5 says, "Keep your lives free from the love of money and be content with what you have, because God has said, 'Never will I leave you; never will I forsake you.' " It is a powerful opportunity that God can use to free us from the love of money. No one wants to think we love money or material things too much, but if we can't give it up, we probably do.

I have learned so much in my victories and my failures throughout the challenge.

Here were some thoughts from Day 1:

1. I love how limitations force creativity. The weather was warmer than usual, and although my winter wardrobe is fine, my warmer wardrobe for my current figure (which is not exactly the same as last summer) is not great. Day 1, and I already was thinking, *I need to get new clothes!* I ended up finding something new to pair together. And ironically, it started raining while we were walking into church. I got pretty soaked and was quickly reminded that had I had on the perfect new outfit, I would have been just as drenched and probably frustrated that a new outfit could so quickly lose its luster.

2. I noticed my limitations with my wardrobe have lowered my expectations for how I dressed. Knowing spending is possible means there is always this subconscious higher standard to achieve. And if you have money to spend, you are always striving for it. When you can't spend the money, you just kind of decide it doesn't matter. No more striving. I'm okay wearing the same thing over and over again. The thought is incredibly freeing. I think this is one reason the poor days of a young marriage can seem so sweet.

3. I want to live free. The sermon title for today, this Day 1 of my challenge, was "Unshackled." How incredibly fitting. I tell y'all, God is hitting me at all angles with this message of a life of freedom that can only come when *things* are not my answer.

4. Coco Chanel was on to something when she coined the idea of always taking off one accessory before you leave the house. I am stealing this for my shopping habits. I had to buy Vivi a few things because she is growing like a weed. They were necessities, but hopping online to buy "necessities" is normally my gateway drug to buying the cute white Keds I just noticed or maybe a bathing suit and a much pricier pair of PJs than are really necessary. As I mentioned, online shopping is my weakness, and the few necessities in my cart would have justified all my purchases. This time at checkout, I deleted four things from my cart. It was sad. (She would have looked so cute in the Keds.) But so liberating. I didn't need to buy them to be happy, and that made me very happy! So next time you are about to check out, think of Coco Chanel and see if there is anything you can delete!

Around two months in, the wheels started falling off the wagon. I didn't realize what an all-or-nothing gal I was, but as soon as I justified one purchase, I was able to justify all of them.

We headed to Old Navy to buy Vivi some $2 flip flops. Harmless, right? There's no getting to the kid's section without passing by the women's clothes. Unless of course you walk through the men's section, but that would have meant I wouldn't have been able to innocently pass the women's clothes. I must have forgotten how inexpensive Old Navy was, because the 2 for $15 signs were like runway lights. *Oh I could definitely use a few t-shirts to work out in. Maybe then I'd work out?* That was semi-justifiable. A legitimate excuse I use to not work out is not having clean workout clothes because I have so little. Then there was a dress. And Easter was just around the corner. I justified it, y'all. I justified the heck out of it. I wanted to feel pretty. I never felt pretty anymore. Everything I had for spring and summer didn't fit anyway. I had a strong case, so into the cart it went. Then we headed to get the flip-flops . . . and an Easter dress for Vivi. Things were snowballing fast. The biggest irony is, our family didn't even go to church on Easter because we were all sick. Contentment Challenge: 1. Easter Dress: Goose Egg.

Not a week later, I was the proud new owner of a bunch of new essential oils that were, in fact, non-essential. I had decided I should create a capsule wardrobe for spring and summer, so I had clothes that were comfortable and *oh look! J. Crew has my favorite shorts on sale.* And possibly the easiest thing I could have avoided, two pots for our indoor plants . . . from Target. It was the obvious unjustifiable offender that I had literally listed in my examples of things not to spend money on. Two weeks of weak-willed decisions will do that to you, though.

Why am I telling you all this if it didn't work? Because this is the thought process. This is where the breakdown happens. Maybe if we realize the pitfalls, we will be stronger to fight them.

One thing that really struck me was when all this started happening. It was right around the time we were getting sick and weak in so many ways. We have moments of weakness where fighting temptation is harder than normal. Satan uses a few different tactics.

1 John 2: 15-17 (NASB) says, "Do not love the world nor the things in the world. If anyone loves the world, the love of the Father is not in him. For all that is in the world, the lust of the flesh and the lust of the eyes and the boastful pride of life, is not from the Father, but is from the world. The world is passing away, and also its lusts; but the one who does the will of God lives forever."

These desires that Satan uses—the lust of flesh (taste, touch, smell, and sound), the lust of the eyes (sight), and the pride of life (pride, selfishness)—all tug at something different in us. Where are your moments of weakness? When do you find yourself completely ready to give in to temptation?

Charles Stanley talks about four times when we are most susceptible to temptation: when we are tired, lonely, angry, and hungry. When we are tired of shopping all day long and still can't find the right dress, we will drop big bucks for a half-decent one that we'd normally never buy. When we are bored and lonely, we grab our computer and shop. When we are angry, we think a splurge will cool us down. When we grocery shop hungry, we grab things we would normally be able to resist.

Temptations were made to look appealing. If they weren't, we wouldn't fall for them. But they are, and they make choosing the wise thing hard. When two choices arise like buy that shirt or pass it up, I want to remember to reject the euphoria that moment of spending can bring and remind myself of the reality.

We buy because we think it will satisfy. I'm not talking about a phone charger we need. You know your shopping demons: the home goods at Target, the new shirt from the boutique, the latest book you won't actually read, the $20 cheese from Whole Foods, etc. Those things lose power when we can accurately define them.

Put a value on that thing that is calling your name. And not just a dollar sign. We have to assign it a value for what it means in our lives. Is this _____ worth _____ hours of work? Will this really help me get the results I expect it to give? If I can visualize something a month down the road, what is it doing? Is it truly transforming how I do things, or is it sitting in a closet unused?

I don't want to be a collector of things but of memories. Memories take up no physical space and have the power to make me smile for decades. It's simple really—focus on people instead of things. Fill up emotional tanks instead of shopping carts. Why do we make it so complicated?

At the end of the day and at the end of our life, we can't take it with us. We know that. But I sure cling to my things like I don't know that. Here is the reality: 1 Timothy 6:6-10 says, "But godliness with contentment is great gain. For we brought nothing into the world, and we can take nothing out of it. But if we have food and clothing, we will be content with that. Those who want to get rich fall into temptation and a trap and into many foolish and harmful desires that plunge people into ruin and destruction. For the love of money is a root of all kinds of evil. Some people, eager for money, have wandered from the faith and pierced themselves with many griefs." There is great gain in godliness with contentment. I think by now we all know that gain is not stuff.

I have shared several ways I failed miserably at this whole contentment thing, but there is one example where I believed the truth and it prevailed over my desire for more.

It all started the year we were debating whether to build a home or buy something already built. I began picturing a beautiful home and not wanting anyone to touch or spill on anything. I realized that this wasn't the cozy picture I had dreamed of for us and our guests. So from there we decided our things wouldn't be expensive, our couch would be washable, and our home would be livable.

I also started thinking about the envy I had when I saw beautiful house pictures. Although I had been a little set on building our own home so we could incorporate everything we wanted, I flip flopped and got consumed with the idea that I wanted something less than new and something that wasn't even perfect for us. Instead I wanted something that had imperfections so that we could experience joy not dependent on perfect circumstances. It was such a weird feeling for sure. I wanted a comfortable place, yes, but didn't want to inspire envy like I had felt. Instead, I wanted to inspire peace and joy.

So as we tabled building our own home, we remembered a family that would be moving soon from their home in the neighborhood we dreamed of living. Their house was seven years old. Not old by any standards but not the blank canvas I originally envisioned. The spot was perfect, right across from big old oak trees, but we had little idea what it looked like besides having viewed the floor plan. It was truly amazing to decide before we even saw the house that my expectations were no longer for perfect and pristine. We didn't need to look at the fixtures or even the layout to know that we could be content there. When we did look at it, our decision had already been made. What we saw was perfect for us even though technically the kitchen didn't face the dining or there was no island or office and the master closet was smaller than most. It was perfect. This is the power of contentment. It turned what was before us into enough. Actually, better then enough. Perfect.

HOMEWORK

WORK IT OUT

Grab your *Lessons from The Finishing School* workbook
or your worksheet, A GUIDE TO CONTENTMENT,
from the website and let the refining begin!

RECOMMENDED RESOURCES

SATISFIED
book by jeff manion

CONTENTMENT CHALLENGE
nancyrayphotography.com/my-contentment-story

Find links to the worksheet and extra resources at
VALMARIEPAPER. COM /HOMEWORK.
password: fairlady

16

I Heart Tech

A GUIDE TO INFLUENCE

I spent a summer in Philadelphia while in college interning at a magazine. The experience taught me so much about my future career. Although I loved the idea of designing features in glossy magazines, VIP parties and using words like "nosh" were just not for me.

Every day as I left the city to head to my aunt and uncle's house in the 'burbs, I passed a homeless man named Steve. He was probably in his fifties, but the sun had aged him and he looked much older. His shoulders were leathery and brown, all of which I could see because he wore no shirt. After seeing him a few days in a row, I decided I'd start keeping a bottle of water and granola bar in my car so I could give it to him on those days when I caught the red light he was at. I did this for a few weeks, catching him a few times. Then I decided I wanted to do a little more. Since he had no shirt, I dug through my things and found one from school that was a little big for me and would fit his small frame. It was cornflower blue and read, "I heart Tech" with a big red heart instead of the word (I love NY shirts were all the rage at the time).

I threw it in the car and gave it to my new friend the next time I passed him. He wasn't quite as enthused as I pictured, but I still felt good about my little deed. Leaving work that day, I couldn't wait to see if Steve had his shiny new shirt on. As I pulled close, I could see he had a shirt on! Yay! What a blessing to have a little shield from the sun. And then as I got closer, I noticed it wasn't MY shirt. It was some plain white t-shirt that was full of holes.

I felt totally bamboozled. Did Steve have a closet full of clothes and just didn't like wearing shirts? The wind left my sails. I was a self-consumed kid who had finally shown a little human compassion and had started to feel like I wasn't making any difference at all.

I didn't see him for a while. He must have moved to a new stop light that I didn't pass. Then one day, I did recognize him in a new location. Or rather, I recognized his shirt. There it was, a cornflower blue "I heart Tech" shirt. I started crying hysterically. He was wearing my shirt. We don't always get to see the impact we make, but when we do, it can be so motivating. It was a small thing to give a shirt away, but for this twenty-year-old, my heart felt the joy that came from doing something for someone else, and from that point forward, I was able to really believe what I had heard all along that "it's better to give than to receive."

A few days before I left Philly to head back to school, my family came up, and we were going to take the train to New York for my sister's and my twenty-first birthday. Before we left, we went to see the magazine I worked at, and on the way home, we saw Steve. We stopped at the Wal-Mart, got him some clothes and a jacket for the harsh winter that was coming, a few toiletries, food, a Burger King gift card, and a Bible.

As sweet as the story was for me and as much as I learned about being available to say yes to God, I still have days when I wake up with no expectations for my day. I forget that I can make a difference. Then there are other days I wake up with hope and these, y'all, these are the days that I live for.

What if we woke up each morning anticipating God to use us and do great things in us? What if we expected it? Our eyes would be opened to all the opportunities that might have always been before us but we were too distracted to see. I pray every morning that God gives me eyes to see the needs around me. Some days I see them, and some days I totally miss out because I'm too focused on me.

I have come to recognize several pitfalls that can hold us back from changing this world.

OUR OWN COMFORTS

One book that has totally inspired me to be available for God moments was *Love, Skip, Jump* by Shelene Bryan. She includes dozens of God stories that will have you saying, "I want to be a part of something like that!" And y'all, we can if we simply say yes to God. The more we say yes, the more God can entrust us with. And the more we say no, the less He sends our way or, at the very least, the better we get at ignoring those promptings from God to make a difference to someone.

Shelene says, "We are not seeing God because in our self-created 'Christianity-Lite' world, we are not trying anything that only God can do. We have designed our lives so that He never needs to step in . . . What are you doing in your life right now that you could not do without the power of almighty God? If you can't answer that, there is a good chance you feel distant from Him."

Christianity Lite. Is that how you are living? I know I live this way a lot. I get comfortable in my little bubble. I like my safe space and consistency and operate just fine serving others from it. But I don't see miracles on a regular basis or get to be a part of God's bigger story and purpose for my life when I am ignoring His opportunities. And let's be honest, we are all carrying our own load. We don't really have time to stop for even five minutes because we are always headed somewhere important, right?

Shelene talks about recognizing our comforts that constrain our desire to follow God. After reading the previous chapters, you have probably guessed I love my comforts. I love pepperoni pizza and don't stray far from it. It's a comfort to me. But are your comforts and my comforts holding us back from being a part of God's story?

Sometimes I'm inspired to pray a scary prayer. I pray for God to disrupt my day. He knows better than me the needs around me, and I actually ask Him to hijack my schedule or plans for the day. Sometimes I say this reluctantly because what I have to do feels really important and I'd rather not have to scratch anything out in my planner or even worse, not get to check something off. But I pray it anyway, knowing God has the best plan for me. I do this because I have experienced the joy that comes with serving and making a difference, and I crave it.

OUR PRIDE AND SELFISHNESS

Some people are tough to serve and—being the big shot I am (in my head)—I think it's up to me to pick and choose whom to serve. I'll welcome the girl like me who just joined the club but not the one who is a few degrees from my definition of normal. Well this is embarrassing. Shouldn't we love all His kids?

Matthew 25:34-40 tells us,

> Then the King will say to those on his right, "Come, you who are blessed by my Father, inherit the kingdom prepared for you from the foundation of the world. For I was hungry and you gave me food, I was thirsty and you gave me drink, I was a stranger and you welcomed me, I was naked and you clothed me, I was sick and you visited me, I was in prison and you came to me." Then the righteous will answer him, saying, 'Lord, when did we see you hungry and feed

you, or thirsty and give you drink? And when did we see you
a stranger and welcome you, or naked and clothe you? And
when did we see you sick or in prison and visit you?" And
the King will answer them, "Truly, I say to you, as you did
it to one of the least of these my brothers, you did it to me."

This reminds me to stop being the judge and jury and value all
God's children and serve in whatever opportunities God gives me.
That actually makes this whole thing pretty simple, if you ask me.

OUR INSECURITIES

No matter how inadequate we feel, God is not looking for perfect
or even near perfect people to use. He just needs willing hearts,
and He can do the rest. Our insecurities can hold us back from
serving because we feel ill-equipped, but the Bible is filled with
people who would never pass the first round of many of the tasks
they were asked to do. They did it because God called on them.
They said yes, and He provided the strength for it.

God can use you. Four years ago, I was consumed with myself
and had one thing in mind: my sweet husband and my business.
God opened my heart, and I don't even know how he did it, to be
honest. I do remember some close people in my life (ahem, Mom
and Nan?) who just flat out told me I was selfish. It was while we
were planning our wedding, and my answer was that I didn't think
I was and if I was, I had a right to be. I was busy.

That hit me pretty hard. You never want anyone to think you
are selfish. I still don't think I went up to God and said, "Hey I
don't want to be selfish. Can you help me?" I think He just saw a
crack in the door and came in. He had me praying prayers about
opening my eyes so I could see the needs around me before I even
knew what that meant. Since then, He has given me so many op-

portunities to be a part of so many stories. I don't share this because I did anything special. Not at all actually. My hope is that you walk away knowing that it doesn't matter where you have been. God wants to use you for His kingdom if you are open to it.

OUR FIXATION ON OTHERS

God will use us if we are willing. I find sometimes that it's not that I'm unwilling, but I don't feel like can do much. I love to think that if I had the audience of Taylor Swift, I could do amazing things with it. I'd talk less about boys and more about God and influence MILLIONS. I am so not hating on Taylor. Vivi and I love dancing to her music, but if i was hating on her, I'd just tell her to listen to that catchy tune "Shake It Off" and she'd be fine. Alas, I don't have an audience of millions, so I'll just drink my tea and watch my Frasier reruns because, like I said in not so many words, I can't make a difference without the ears of millions of people.

It's of course a subconscious thought I'm letting become conscious now for the sake of this chapter. I would normally never utter such a thing, but my actions can tell a different story.

Does not having a big platform discourage you like it can discourage me? And what is big anyways? If we can't make really big things happen, a lot of times we bow out of doing anything at all. The world seems too big. There are too many starving children, too many homeless people, too many victims of (insert the cause you are passionate about). It's just too dang much to tackle.

Why in my head do I think all or nothing? Part of me thinks it's my pride oozing out. What would be demeaning about helping one homeless person? The answer is nothing. But how many people would get to look at me and see all the good I was doing? Maybe no one. And sometimes unfortunately that's enough to take me out of the running.

One book that has been so refreshing to read on this topic is *Clout* by Jenni Catron. She says, "Envy is one of the greatest distractions to our influence. It takes our focus off our opportunities for influence and tempts us to fixate on everyone else's."

I see all the gifts my friends are equipped with or, better yet, the things it looks like they get handed to them, and I get sidetracked. I wish I could do what they are doing, and in all this daydreaming and wishing, I don't do the things I was meant to do. God has a different plan for all of us. What's His plan for you? Are you living it out?

When we do good and no one sees, God sees. Gosh, Val, that's nothing new. I know, I know. But if you forget God's simplest teachings like I do, you might need the reminder too. This goes back to Colossians 3:23 (ESV), "Whatever you do, work heartily, as for the Lord and not for men." We may only have an audience of one, but it is the single greatest audience we could ever have.

Is there anything wrong with having an audience of millions? Absolutely not. And that's not totally out of the question for you to have one day, but what are you doing right now with the hundred people who are listening to you and seeing you? Don't waste the opportunities we have today because we have convinced ourselves that they are too small to matter.

The Bible clearly says in Luke 16:10, "Whoever can be trusted with very little can also be trusted with much, and whoever is dishonest with very little will also be dishonest with much."

If you want to influence the world, start right where you are. Show the Lord you are willing to point to His kingdom even if only three people (most probably your mom and dad and best friend) are listening. I am not going to tell you how to gain influence with others because truthfully, you already have it. Someone around you is seeing your life and being influenced by it, good or bad. So the question is: How are we using this influence? Or are we using it at all?

HOMEWORK

WORK IT OUT

Grab your *Lessons from The Finishing School* workbook
or your worksheet, A GUIDE TO INFLUENCE,
from the website and let the refining begin!

RECOMMENDED RESOURCES

LOVE, SKIP, JUMP
book by shelene bryan

CLOUT
book by jenni catron

INFLUENCE NETWORK
online community - theinfluencenetwork.com

Find links to the worksheet and extra resources at
VALMARIEPAPER.COM/HOMEWORK
password: fairlady

17

Serman Hall Pass

A GUIDE TO FORGIVENESS

In the past, when sermons on forgiveness would happen, the pastor would inevitably ask you to think about someone you needed to forgive. This is when I could kick back, maybe look through the maps in my Bible or even my Instagram if I was feeling particularly brazen, because I couldn't think of anyone I needed to forgive. I basically earned myself a free period for the next thirty minutes and could sit this one out.

Then one day, the inevitable happened. Someone wronged me. Not only that, but she couldn't admit it and didn't apologize or ask forgiveness. I like to tell myself if she had, I could have forgiven easily, so this was pretty much her fault and another item to heap on my pile of reasons to be bitter. My stomach was in knots for days; I couldn't sleep and suddenly regretted tuning out those sermons on forgiveness.

Months went by, and things slowly got better. Then I'd have days where all the hurt resurfaced and felt as fresh as the day it happened. I prayed through this time, but I really needed practical guidance for how to change my heart on this matter. I wanted to open my heart up and actively pursue God's plan for me and not keep sitting around waiting for a forgiveness pill to be invented.

Maybe next year, scientists.

I decided to study God's Word for verses and stories on bitterness and freedom. As I opened my heart for God to work, He began to show me how unforgiving I can be for the littlest things. Traffic made me curse, and my lack of grace for others meant I was harboring so much unsettled strife in my heart. There was no huge issue, just a heart that had trouble understanding grace enough to forgive others and myself.

I didn't want bitterness; I wanted freedom. I didn't want to keep tallies, I wanted to love freely. If you have ever held on to unforgiveness for long, you know it can be exhausting. I was tired of being tired. I was ready to feel energized by relationships.

One passage that gave me a fresh perspective was Colossians 3:12-17. Beyond the short line or two actually talking about forgiveness, the passage is full of wisdom on living a life free from bitterness and secrets to living well with others.

> Therefore, as God's chosen people, holy and dearly loved, clothe yourselves with compassion, kindness, humility, gentleness and patience. Bear with each other and forgive one another if any of you has a grievance against someone. Forgive as the Lord forgave you. And over all these virtues put on love, which binds them all together in perfect unity.
>
> Let the peace of Christ rule in your hearts, since as members of one body you were called to peace. And be thankful. Let the message of Christ dwell among you richly as you teach and admonish one another with all wisdom through psalms, hymns, and songs from the Spirit, singing to God with gratitude in your hearts. And whatever you do, whether in word or deed, do it all in the name of the Lord Jesus, giving thanks to God the Father through him.

Forgive as the Lord forgives? How does the Lord forgive? I'm so glad you asked! The Message version for this passage says to forgive quickly and completely.

Quickly. How often have I taken my time to forgive and kind of left it up to simply the passing of days for the sting to wear off to forgive someone? Once the wound isn't so fresh, it can definitely be easier to forgive, right? Get ready to have your toes trampled. Jesus forgave us and all those who nailed Him to a cross while His wounds were fresh and gaping open. Just imagining that makes my own blood boil for Him, and it is so hard to comprehend how He forgave in that moment. But this is the example we have and we can't ignore that.

Completely. How often have I held on to some piece of bitterness and not let it go completely? Sometimes I feel like I do this because I'm afraid that I'm justifying their actions or saying it was okay for them to hurt me. If I hold on to a little piece of it, I am continuing to acknowledge that they wronged me. It seems less naive. As I think more about my reasons for holding on to the hurt, I have to ask myself a really blunt and what I wish was an obvious question but something I usually forget: what is my purpose for not forgiving? Surely I have a logical reason! Do I do it to cause someone else pain or to teach them a lesson? If so, I may want to change my strategy, because normally that person doesn't even know the strife I'm putting my heart through.

There is someone else who loves to see us harbor unforgiveness, and that guy goes by the name of Satan. He wants our hearts to fester with unforgiveness. Have you met anyone who was holding on to a hurt for years? It corrodes them. It steals their joy and imprisons them by calling them back to strife and tension. Satan has a field day. He wants to see us so distracted and unhappy that we can't experience God's full grace.

And without understanding God's grace for me, I will struggle to love fully, to free my heart from bitterness. Hebrews 12:15 (ESV) says, "See to it that no one fails to obtain the grace of God, that no 'root of bitterness' springs up and causes trouble, and by it many become defiled."

Understanding God's grace has been a twenty-five-year battle for me. I got saved at the ripe age of six and was a good girl (dare I say great girl) for my kid to teenage life and beyond. You can ask my parents. The worst thing they had to deal with was "an attitude problem" when I was a tween. This consisted of whining and wanting my parents to buy me name-brand clothes. Not Gap or even Limited Too. I'm talking of course about Umbro and Adidas. And there was that one time I snuck out of my house around midnight to hang out in the driveway with a blue-haired boy and get my very first kiss. They had no need to punish me. I received my punishment in full when my first kiss was not as epic as Jamie and Landon's in *A Walk to Remember* and there was no "Dancing in the Moonlight" playing in the background as I would have preferred.

Growing up a good girl has its own issues. I wasn't living with guilt or shame for things I had done. I was battling pride in my heart and legalism. The God I knew blessed you for the right things you did and cursed you for the bad things. If something bad happened to someone, I immediately tried to discern what that person had done wrong to cause it. I even have moments still where I have to fight this thinking.

One incredible story in the Bible that reminds me of God's grace for me is the parable found in Matthew 18 of the ruler who forgave the debt of one of the citizens. It was a huge debt. After this guy's debt was forgiven, meaning all record was wiped away and he no longer owed it, he went to someone who owed him a very small amount and railed him for not having his money. This seems like such an extreme and obvious example. What a cruel person it must take to forget how much he has been forgiven and demand so much more from someone else. I winced a little when I was brought back to reality and realized that is exactly like God's forgiveness for us and our struggles to forgive those who hurt us. To me, the hurts I feel are huge, but when I hold it up to the forgiveness God has shown me, it pales millionfold in comparison. Being reminded of the mercy poured out on me helps me to keep perspective and to let go of those things a little better.

Forgiveness is still a work in progress, though. We can be reminded of things that happened and feel bitterness creep in. This doesn't necessarily mean we didn't forgive when we thought we did. It just may mean that it's something we have to keep bringing back to God. Also in Matthew 18, when Jesus told Paul to forgive someone seventy times seven (which basically means just keep forgiving), I wonder if sometimes that's not referring to the same issue that we might need to let go of more than once. My study of forgiveness led me to three hard truths to remember:

1. Good works are worthless if we don't love others. This morning's sermon at church was on the parables found in Luke 18. The Pharisee in the parable was praying and basically saying he was so glad he was good and not like the tax collector (who happened to be in earshot). The Pharisee had a long list of truly good works. He wasn't a fake guy. He really did the work. BUT, and there is a big one, when we look at that famous love passage, specifically 1 Corinthians 13:1-3 (ESV), we are reminded that those good works are useless if we treat others poorly. "If I speak in the tongues of men and of angels, but have not love, I am a noisy gong or a clanging cymbal. And if I have prophetic powers, and understand all mysteries and all knowledge, and if I have all faith, so as to remove mountains, but have not love, I am nothing. If I give away all I have, and if I deliver up my body to be burned, but have not love, I gain nothing."

Can my lifelong Bible readers back me up on this? Did y'all remember that's what this passage meant? I don't think I have read this passage in a non-wedding setting in years. It is rich with meaning, but the meaning was lost on me as I primped my hair or noticed all the things me, a former wedding planner, would have done differently (AKA better) for the wedding ceremony. This is a tough truth. Stop striving for a good deed here and good deed there if you can't love that person who hurt you six months ago. I feel all bossy even typing it, but goodness. It's pretty straightforward, and as much as I'd like to soften it so you can all go tell your friends what an "uplifting read" this book was, I've got to share truth with you. And also, I warned you. These bullet points are called "hard truths" for a reason. This good girl is squirming in her seat. I valued my good works so much, and if I'm being honest, I valued them above people a lot of times. To hear that they were basically worthless without loving others was a reality check. I know people are important to God, blah blah blah. I've heard that a thousand times, but to hear it this way made me see how real this was.

2. The measure you use for others will be used for you.
Don't shoot the messenger on this one either. Luke 6 (ESV) say this:

> Judge not, and you will not be judged; condemn not, and you will not be condemned; forgive, and you will be forgiven; give, and it will be given to you. Good measure, pressed down, shaken together, running over, will be put into your lap. For with the measure you use it will be measured back to you.

Y'all, what if we started racking up some forgiveness points instead of getting angry at every offense knowing we will indeed do something stupid one day and need forgiveness ourselves? Probably today, actually. You know it doesn't really work like that, but could we shift our brain to simply forgive knowing we screw up too? I sure hope you said yes, because it is basically the golden rule. Do unto to others as you would have them do unto you. And I'll wager anything that you would want others to forgive you.

3. If I can't forgive myself, I can't forgive others. We have to get this concept of grace. I have already mentioned I struggle fully understanding it. When I mess up, my gut reaction is to expect the consequence around the corner, or when something doesn't go favorably, I am quick to figure out what I did wrong to cause it. But how can we understand God's love and offering others grace if we don't accept the grace that has been given to us?

I love what Lysa TerKeurst said in her book *Unglued* about this: "It is beautiful when the Master chisels. God doesn't allow the unglued moments of our lives to happen so we'll label ourselves and stay stuck. He allows the unglued moments to make us aware of the chiseling that needs to be done. So instead of condemning myself with statements like, I'm such a mess, I could say, Let God chisel."

God is still at work in us. Ephesians 2:10 calls us His workmanship. As you read God's Word, look for pictures of His grace. Hint: they are all over the place. A great passage to start with is John 8:1-11. When we understand grace, forgiveness can flow easier from us. It's not something we are kicking and screaming to do because we personally have it. It's ours to give away freely.

I am sitting on the front row preaching this to myself right now. Honestly, this lesson is hard and I wish I had five foolproof steps to forgiveness, but I don't. All I know is that I want to keep God's truth that I learned and shared in this chapter in front of my eyes and written on my heart.

H O M E W O R K

WORK IT OUT

Grab your *Lessons from The Finishing School* workbook
or your worksheet, A GUIDE TO FORGIVENESS,
from the website and let the refining begin!

RECOMMENDED RESOURCES

*THE FREEDOM OF
SELF-FORGETFULNESS*
book by timothy keller

Find links to the worksheet and extra resources at
VALMARIEPAPER.COM/HOMEWORK.
password: fairlady

18

Buried in the Sand

A GUIDE TO AWARENESS

This chapter is the class you took your last semester of school because you dreaded it and were kind of hoping they would change the requirements before you had to take it. No such luck, my friends. We've got some learning to do.

For me, that dreaded class was speech. That class was a major victory for me and still so vivid. I remember doing an argumentative speech on why organic food was not necessarily better than conventional. I had been interning at the local newspaper around that time and had to write a story about why organic food was so great. The thing was, the sources couldn't really say why. The best they could come up with was some scare tactics, and this didn't fly with me.

Thankfully, I made sure to state in my presentation that my argument was based on current findings that way I wouldn't look like a total moron when this whole organic thing gained some legs. But this situation had me thinking: are we educating ourselves or even using any common sense at all with today's issues? I still can't believe young Valerie could be so wise as to look for the facts through the fluff. I sure hope you hold on to that sweet girl in your head, because an example of present-day Valerie is coming. And it ain't pretty.

I remember all too recently thinking about the fact that we didn't recycle. It made me feel laid back like I'd be chill if our air got "a little toxic-y." I'd rather be putting out a little waste than ever be called uptight or high maintenance. And at the same time, I thought I was too busy with "important" things to make time to rummage through my garbage trying to decide what to recycle. We had souls to save! Aren't they more important than APB or what's that bad material called?

There is absolutely no logic in that. None. But it was easier to believe that than do something or even pull out my laptop and do the research. The more I found out, the scarier the world of products got, and the more overwhelming it seems to try to keep the toxins at bay. I'm pretty much eating them, wearing them, bathing in them, and inhaling them. Most days it's easier to worry about Pinterest projects and our kids needing new clothes or grades on a test. We block out the rest of the world and live in our comfortable bubble of a town called Simple Living, USA.

What areas have you chosen to be naive about? With what issues do you completely bury your head in the sand because they overwhelm you or you don't know what you could possibly do to help? For you it might be politics or sex-trafficking. It might even be parenting.

The world needs all of us to stop ignoring things because they are too hard and uncomfortable. We have lost our grip on reality—that people actually die from not having enough food, that people die because they believe in Jesus, and that people die from chemicals and things man made and says are okay to use. The world is fallen. We shouldn't be crippled by it, and we shouldn't ignore it.

This chapter was not something I planned to write. I fell into it because learning how to be aware of the world around me is something I need to hear and learn. I'm uncomfortable just writing this chapter and would honestly rather get back to writing about studying the Bible. I am much more comfortable with that.

But in the same way we can't pick and choose which pages of the Bible we will keep, we can't pick and choose what is reality around us. And how can we possibly make a positive impact in the world if we don't learn about it?

Right now, I'm digging deep into this green thing. It's something I have ignored for too long and pretend like it's just for hippies or Portland folks. Somewhere along the line, green living became associated with anyone but Christians. Have you thought about the fact that people who don't even believe in God are taking better care of His Creation than His own kids?

Colossians 1:15-16 says, "Jesus is the image of the invisible God, the firstborn of all creation; for in him all things in heaven and on earth were created, things visible and invisible, whether thrones or dominions or rulers or powers—all things have been created through him and for him."

When I'm looking at a mountain, I can appreciate that God created the earth. But when I'm taking the trash out on Thursday night for pickup in the morning, I am not for one second thinking about this earth God created.

To be honest, taking care of our environment is my easy answer to awareness. I'll start recycling and reading labels better. I can do that from the safety of my home. But do you get as uncomfortable as I do when people talk of Christians dying in other countries? I read an article that someone linked to on Facebook about all the Christians being killed around the world, complete with images of them being led like dogs to their execution. It was disturbing, and I don't like to be disturbed. That article caused me so much fear. Here is my initial struggle: What good does it do me to be aware of these things that I can't control? Why not just turn off my news and not live in fear?

You heard me talk about all the trouble I have had with my

ears. I have clung to this passage during every ear episode I've had for fifteen years. 2 Corinthians 1:8-10 says, "We do not want you to be uninformed, brothers and sisters, about the troubles we experienced in the province of Asia. We were under great pressure, far beyond our ability to endure, so that we despaired of life itself. Indeed, we felt we had received the sentence of death. But this happened that we might not rely on ourselves but on God, who raises the dead. He has delivered us from such a deadly peril, and he will deliver us again. On him we have set our hope that he will continue to deliver us."

I related this to my ears when they talk about a great pressure so similar to the ear pressure I felt that caused me agony. Then I leaned on God's truth about why this happened: "that we might not rely on ourselves but on God, who raises the dead." This portion always had me do an about-face from stewing in my fear to putting my trust in God. But what I just noticed about this passage was the very first eight words that I have glazed passed a thousand times: "we do not want you to be uninformed." This band of believers, no matter how far they are, are the church. We are all a part of God's family. And God uses us being informed to change us as well.

I have been reading about the start of the church in Acts, and I feel such a sense of excitement as I read. Lives are being changed; there is a gusto in their bones. Their numbers were growing, their faith was growing, and they took care of each other. It just seems like it would have been a cool time to be a part of the church. And it was, but there was also heavy persecution during this time and lots of bloodshed. I go back to 2 Corinthians and think about that pressure and what we know about pearls and how it's from the pressure that such beauty is created. Our current times reveal this every day. As we face silent judgment or rude comments in America, instead of execution, we become lukewarm for the Lord. Those people that have to choose between saving their life or proclaiming Jesus have a fire for the Lord that is white hot and furthermore, it's spreading like wildfire. Our pastor said that the Southern hemisphere is exploding for Jesus, specifically areas that make it difficult to be a Christian.

If we decide to keep out those things that are uncomfortable to hear about, we also keep out the God-sized stories taking place. How do we get past the fear and become aware and use that awareness? Fear is simply not a good reason to ignore it. We are conveniently talking about peace next, so hold tight. For now, I will answer my initial question: what good does it do me to be aware of these things that I can't control? And what can I do to help?

1. To bring awareness to others with the intent to make a difference. We can't control it, but we can do something. What is your passion? What issue do you want to bring more awareness to? The world needs you. I recently found out about an organization, Exile International, that provides art therapy and rehabilitative care in Uganda and DR Congo to restore former child soldiers and war-affected children to become leaders for peace. I had no idea this type of help existed and am loving the opportunity to support their efforts. Maybe you need to be the voice that will encourage others to action.

2. To support with our dollar. We have resources here. You don't need a whole song and dance about how we are very rich, even if you don't feel rich, compared to the rest of the world. The fact is, it's God's money that He entrusted you with to use. Maybe some of that money you saved during the contentment challenge can go to support a cause you are passionate about.

3. To support with our voice. Pray. How are us lazy bones not doing at least this one consistently? When we know someone personally who is dying, we rally the troops to pray for them. Can we do the same for our brothers and sisters around the world? A few things I have been praying for lately are: asking God to give them an assurance of His presence with them and boldness and asking God to bring comfort and even peace through their trials.

4. To offer compassion and understanding. After the events in Baltimore that followed Freddie Gray's death, I had some real conversations about race. A black Christian sister said she felt white Christians were supporting blacks in other countries but ignoring the issues here. I wanted her to be wrong, but she wasn't. I had let fear of my support being misunderstood stop me from saying anything. Our silence translates to lack of respect. Creating a dialogue is so important. You may not turn the tide of race for the world, but you can make sure the people you come into contact with feel loved and heard.

5. To encourage our own faith. Do you think the people Paul wrote to were changed at all by his letters and the trials they heard about? I can't imagine not. But so many times, we don't hear the stories and we don't think they are talking to us, so we aren't changed. When I listen, though, I am reminded of my own lukewarmness and am inspired to live boldly for the Lord. Their unwavering faith should encourage us to shine brighter in a dark world.

I will be the first to say, I don't think awareness comes with just turning on your news for hours and hours a day. I graduated in journalism and worked at my local newspaper for a year after school. Most news is depressing, and I was filling my head with it eight hours a day at work and then going home to watch a couple hours of news. I lived with a lot of fear. I have swung in the completely opposite direction and for a few years didn't listen to any news besides what popped up in my Facebook feed. Neither are the answer.

If you are particularly fearful, too much news can have you feeling like you strapped a water hose to your mouth. It's just too much to take in at once. Start slow and always pair it with time in the Word. We have to combat that fear or the overwhelming feelings you feel with God's truth. God's truth should actually overwhelm you. He is King on high who reigns forever and His plan is perfect and good.

HOMEWORK

WORK IT OUT

Grab your *Lessons from The Finishing School* workbook
or your worksheet, A GUIDE TO AWARENESS,
from the website and let the refining begin!

RECOMMENDED RESOURCES

SEVEN
book by jen hatmaker

HOLE IN THE GOSPEL
book by richard stearns

OPERATION WORLD
online guide to world issues - operationworld.org

Find links to the worksheet and extra resources at
VALMARIEPAPER.COM/HOMEWORK
password: fairlady

19

The Pecan

A GUIDE TO PEACE

I have lived in the grips of fear and anxiety, and I have also experienced a peace that can only come from God. It is possible to live free from fear, and I am living proof.

I have already mentioned that fear was my middle name growing up. I had a bad case of hypochondria, so I was having heart attacks at a very early age. I remember getting chest pains in class in high school and immediately thought this was it: I was going to croak right here in computer class. It wasn't heart pains; it was fear that gripped me and sent my heart racing. Being a magician of sorts, I was able to materialize other symptoms to support any diagnosis out of thin air. As a pain in my chest would come on, I would put my head down and pray. I would fill my mind with God's truth and not the lies that I told myself. The pain would subside, and I could come back up for air. My panic attacks could always be remedied by truth because truth cut through the lies that led to my panic attacks in the first place.

Our fears cause us to think the worst. I remember one time as a kid hearing what I thought were steady footsteps coming down the hall while I slept. It turns out, it was our clock ticking. Well, I got over that silly fear only to hear real burglars climbing on the roof above our room! I laid up all night just waiting for them to come to get me. In the morning as I retold the whole harrowing ordeal to my mom, she told me it was squirrels. Squirrels? No way, mom. I did my own detective work and scoured the crime scene, and would you lookee there, it turns out the pecan tree that was ripe for harvest had branches that hung right over our room. I materialized the mix of squirrels scurrying and pecans dropping and rolling down the roof into a very quick-footed and picky burglar. After all, he never actually came inside.

It's amazing what our minds can do. If you are one of those people who thinks you are not creative; if you've got your own pecan story, trust me, you are more creative than you think!

It's funny how God works. Here I was terrified of pecans. I remember this night so vividly. Then I received a bronzed pecan necklace from my husband one Christmas, and the story came full circle. We live in South Louisiana, so bronzing things like pecans or crawfish or other Louisiana-y things is totally normal. I loved it and wore it every day! A few weeks later, we found out I was pregnant. Instead of calling this fetus "the kid" as we had been calling it, we nicknamed it "the pecan." And y'all, this pecan terrified me way more than that one rolling around on the roof. The one rolling around in my belly was one that had caused me fear for years. I honestly wasn't super worried about motherhood. I don't mean that to sound cocky; I just had bigger fish to fry at the time: get through pregnancy, which for a hypochondriac is a hilarious series of events and "what's that?" or "is that supposed to happen?" or "am I dying?"

After a tired and nauseated first trimester, I started walking around the lake by our apartment. I would use this time to pray and give it all up to God. I knew I couldn't do it alone. I think this is the first step to releasing fear: realizing that it's going to take more than anything I've got to give. Until that moment, we try to keep a grasp on it, and it's pretty much a bucking bronco that we cannot tame. As we try to control the situation, the crazier things get, the more out of control we feel. And y'all, we like control. But we have to give it up. Don't expect peace if you are steering the ship. You are blindfolded and yet you still want to drive because you think it will be better than if God drove, someone who is all knowing and all seeing. Truthfully, do I really trust myself more than I trust God? Our pastor talked about a lady whose husband got really sick. She said, "We are so glad we aren't in charge of our life." Because there, she could rest in knowing that she didn't have to have all the answers or even a remedy for the sickness. She trusted God with it. He was in charge.

Do you trust God? That is where peace lies, and He is more than worthy of our trust. Ann Voskamp said, "If God didn't withhold from us His very own Son, will God withhold anything we need? If trust must be earned, hasn't God unequivocally earned our trust with the bark on the raw wounds, the thorns pressed in the brow, your name on the cracked lips?" Turn to His Word and study His character, and you will see a God who cares for us so deeply. He wants only our best and knows exactly what that will be. We don't have to "help" Him out by giving so much attention to our fears of the unknown. They are known by Him. Matthew 6:25-34 illustrates this beautifully.

Therefore I tell you, do not worry about your life, what you will eat or drink; or about your body, what you will wear. Is not life more than food, and the body more than clothes? Look at the birds of the air; they do not sow or reap or store away in barns, and yet your heavenly Father feeds them. Are you not much more valuable than they? Can any one of you by worrying add a single hour to your life? And why do you worry about clothes? See how the flowers of the field grow. They do not labor or spin. Yet I tell you that not even Solomon in all his splendor was dressed like one of these. If that is how God clothes the grass of the field, which is here today and tomorrow is thrown into the fire, will he not much more clothe you—you of little faith? So do not worry, saying, "What shall we eat?" or "What shall we drink?" or "What shall we wear?" For the pagans run after all these things, and your heavenly Father knows that you need them. But seek first his kingdom and his righteousness, and all these things will be given to you as well. Therefore do not worry about tomorrow, for tomorrow will worry about itself. Each day has enough trouble of its own.

Another verse on fear that we like to use a lot is 1 Peter 5:7. It says, "Cast all your anxiety on him because he cares for you." This is great and fabulous, but I've learned context is important. Have you read the rest of the passage? I think it is just as crucial to know. "Be alert and of sober mind. Your enemy the devil prowls around like a roaring lion looking for someone to devour. Resist him, standing firm in the faith, because you know that the family of believers throughout the world is undergoing the same kind of sufferings."

Like so many of the thoughts we talk about in this book that will hold us back, fear is the same. And it's just one more of Satan's tactics to make Christians ineffective. If you are a believer, He is no longer trying to keep you from becoming a Christian, but He will try to make your life as fruitless as possible. Can we remember that fear comes from the devil? That fear is not from God? Have we heard 2 Timothy 1:7 (NLT) too much to believe what it says? "For God has not given us a spirit of fear and timidity, but of power, love, and self-discipline." I feel like I have. It is the fearful person's anthem, and I have sung it for a long time. But as I sit here thinking about what this means, I realize that fear has no place in God's plan for us. It serves no purpose.

So back to pregnant and panicked Valerie. Here I was, completely at the Lord's mercy. I knew I was weak and would likely be hyperventilating into a paper bag daily if it wasn't for a peace that came from letting go. You can ask my husband, my sister, and all those people who know me best—I was the calmest they had ever seen me here when I could have been my most afraid. The version they tell is more like, "Yeah, I was so scared of what a basket case or control freak Valerie was going to be, but she was actually way more calm than she normally is." Thank you, sweet loving family.

Did I do anything beside desperately come to the Father asking for Him to fill my life? Not really. Although I guess there was one thing I did. I didn't just ask for it, but I made space for Him to fill me up. This sounds very hippy dippy, but it just means I spent more time at His feet (or in the Word and in prayer) than I did listening to my fears. You have to turn the fears off. We forget we have the power to do that, but we do. Those fears lie to us. They tell us all sorts of things just to keep us spinning out of control. They want that molehill to turn into a mountain, and all our ruminating and tale spinning and worry will do that. So why do we listen?

As I became a mom, I realized, *Oh I can totally worry about this too*. Each month one of my prayers was "peace for Vivi." This has remained an entry each month because it's something I know I will never be strong enough without the Lord to do on my own. And I am perfectly good with that. In fact, I was boasting in my weakness just like 2 Corinthians 12:9 talks about.

Have you noticed that when you work in your own strength and try to kick and scream your way *out* of a situation, you end up exhausted and anxious? But when you simply trust God and choose to walk THROUGH it connected to Him, you find peace. Psalm 23:4 promises this. "Even though I walk through the darkest valley,

I will fear no evil, for you are with me; your rod and your staff, they comfort me." The Bible is rich in passages about worry as if God is saying, I know you will struggle with fear and I am with you. Here were a few things I've learned from His Word to combat fear and experience peace.

1. Keep your mind set on God's promises. Worries will come in and out, but we need to keep coming back to the promises of God and to remember His goodness and that He sees us and hasn't forgotten us.

2. Remember His past victories. It is incredibly encouraging and peace-giving to know the God I pray to and trust is steadfast, and I have already seen that in my life.

3. Release it to Him. Give Him control and know He is worthy of our trust to let Him lead.

4. Think rationally. You already know most of the things we worry about don't actually happen. And even if they did, our worrying benefits our situation not even a little. Luke 12:25 reminds us of that. "Who of you by worrying can add a single hour to your life?" Worrying doesn't help no matter how much we convince ourselves it will. We have to be rational.

I never thought I would say that I could live free from such anxiety, but I am. Living with peace of course doesn't mean we don't face opportunities to worry. It simply means we don't let it dictate our reaction.

Susan Jeffers says, "Feel the fear and do it anyway." It's in these moments when we choose to do it anyway that we exercise incredible courage. And the more we exercise courage, the easier it becomes. It's like a muscle that gets stronger over time. Smarties of the world all agree that we should do something out of our comfort zone every day. I have had seasons where I experience no uncomfortable moments and can feel my courage retracting. If I am not constantly stretching myself in this way, I forget all too easily that things beyond my comfort zone are possible. Regularly doing this also reminds us that things aren't as bad as we make up in our head most of the time.

"Peace I leave with you; my peace I give to You. Not as the world gives do I give to you. Let not your hearts be troubled, neither let them be afraid." - John 14:27 (ESV)

HOMEWORK

WORK IT OUT

Grab your *Lessons from The Finishing School* workbook
or your worksheet, A GUIDE TO PEACE,
from the website and let the refining begin!

RECOMMENDED RESOURCES

CALM MY ANXIOUS HEART
book by linda dillow

MY NAME IS HOPE
book by john mark comer

Find links to the worksheet and extra resources at
VALMARIEPAPER.COM/HOMEWORK.
password: fairlady

20

You, Me, and the Other Gal
A GUIDE TO COMPARISON

Lot of twins tell stories of how competitive things were when they were kids. It wasn't like that with Natalie and me. I'm not sure why exactly. We were similar for sure, but we had enough differences that we didn't feel the need to compare ourselves. The worst we had was a few friends tell each of us that we were their favorite twin, something that's not fun for either twin to hear actually, but a fact we liked to bring up during fights to hurt the other person.

I got out of high school pretty unscathed, but it's the now that's got me all tangled up in comparison. I find opportunities to compare all around me now as a female entrepreneur with a faith-based creative business in a sea of female entrepreneurs with a faith-based creative business. Let's save some paper by calling them FEs for short. It's hard to fight the thought that your voice isn't needed or that you should be as creative as this gal or as extroverted as this one. It's hard not to see the interaction of their community and not wince a little that yours is not as robust.

The thing is, a lot of these thoughts aren't even true. I made up in my mind that a circle of influential Christian gals had to think my doctrine was false and my advice was terrible. I mentioned this thought to my sister, and she thought I was a ridiculous for even thinking that, in a "how the heck did you materialize that in your mind" sort of way. And that is exactly it. I materialized it. Comparison will do that to you.

Their successes seem to highlight my failures. FE just announced her role in a new project or upcoming event, and you didn't. FE just launched a new line of genius products, and you are working with the same things you've been doing for years. FE just got a thousand million comments on her latest post, and you got only one million.

I have requested my bubble to live in, and so far I haven't received an answer from the big man. Maybe He's trying to teach me another lesson or something, but it looks like He wants me to learn how to live in the world with other FEs.

I love *The Message* version of Galatians 6:4-5, "Make a careful exploration of who you are and the work you have been given, and then sink yourself into that. Don't be impressed with yourself. Don't compare yourself with others. Each of you must take responsibility for doing the creative best you can with your own life."

I honestly couldn't believe it included the words "creative best." It seemed so specific to exactly my struggle, but I know it's a message for all of us. I'm not that vain. There were a few key points I took away from this passage:

1. Stay focused on your own work. This is all about me putting my head down and doing the work God set before me. It's not the bubble of protection I had in mind, but it's something. It's up to me to "sink into" my purpose. How much better would my own work be if I was fully devoted to the purpose set before me and not keeping tabs on everyone else?

2. We are responsible for our own actions. I think if I always remembered that, I would spend a little less time keeping up with everyone else's progress and concentrate on my own work.

3. Nothing pretty comes from comparison. There are only two possible results: we feel like we are worse then someone or we feel like we are better than them. Neither is beneficial.

As I mulled over this idea of comparison, I happened to read (us Bible-thumpers call that "God spoke to me") an enlightening quote from Jen Hatmaker in 7. "I am commissioned to be a light, but I can't illuminate this world while competing with the light of others . . . Together we are a city on a hill. When one of us shines, it is a community victory."

Here I am trying to step on other people to try to pass them up or at least be on their playing field to reach the peak of my goal . . . which is the exact same goal as that person I'm trying to beat: to be a light in the world.

I'm not talking about turning a blind eye to a lack of integrity. Nothing annoys me more than justifying copying off another designer with the phrase "but it's all for God's glory." What glorifies God is honesty and integrity. But that's another sermon for another soapbox.

What I do think is that I should be celebrating in the success of all those gals whom I admire so much and secretly wish I could be as influential as. I should be celebrating that they are reaching people for God. We share a mission, and their advancement of the message should not be seen as a direct blow to me. It's a community victory as Jen calls it. And for this go-round, I'll be the one helping lift up someone on our shoulders as we parade them around the field.

I can't speak for that person who has a job in corporate America and your competition is Susie Sinner. I've been there before, but it has been years. I just remember being super judgy and assuming I'd be better for the job. But oh, what a position we are in to show God's love and exercise humility. Imagine the witness as we serve and express joy even when things don't go as we plan. Joy in trials makes people think, *Huh? Why is she so happy right now?* That is an incredible opportunity to point people to God.

For the stay-at-home mom who has hundreds of mom friends on Facebook, it might be difficult not to use their kid's growth as a measure for your own. Seeing Billy "Quick-Walker" Stevens while your two-month-older girl is still getting her sea legs can make us ask all kinds of questions and wonder if we are doing something wrong. The big question is, am I trying to get the approval of God or man? Galatians 1:10b says, "If I were still trying to please people, I would not be a servant of Christ." Basically, if I'm trying to please people instead of God, I'm looking out for my own agenda and not serving the Lord's purpose.

Any mom worth her salt has uttered to her kids the tear-inducing words, "life's not fair." It's the facts of life. There is a passage in the Bible, that if I'm being particularly argumentative, I'll question until I'm blue in the face. It's the story of the three workers in Matthew 20 (NLT). A man hires a few workers at different times throughout the day and pays them all the same. The one who arrived first is upset because he worked so much longer for the same amount.

> He answered one of them, 'Friend, I haven't been unfair! Didn't you agree to work all day for the usual wage? Take your money and go. I wanted to pay this last worker the same as you. Is it against the law for me to do what I want with my money? Should you be jealous because I am kind to others?'

Here is my big takeaway, which goes back to us running in our own lane. We shouldn't be worried about what other people are getting or not getting. We should be focused on our own race. Should I really be upset when God is generous to a sister? If this worker agreed to work for a certain pay just because someone is getting as much as he is, it is not taking anything away from what the first worker is given.

We all have a different purpose, and God wants to use YOU. Don't let comparison paralyze or keep you from doing what God has planned for you specifically. I love the picture of running in our own lane. Our head is down (or up), but it's not shifting to the sides looking at everyone around us. How can I expect creativity to flow through me if all I'm looking at is other people and trying to be like them? Is it any wonder we all feel so uninspired or uncreative at times? Does this feeling ever hit you? You feel like you have no good ideas left? Or that there is an incredibly lack of individuality all around? I know I have been guilty of this.

Then there are those moments when I have focused on God and simply asked Him to use me, and He has done an amazing work in me. You know how I recognize these moments? When I think about something I have done and think there is no way I could have come up with that on my own.

Just imagine a world where we aren't attempting to be watered-down versions of someone else. Imagine the ideas that would flow! Don't stifle the customized plan God has for your life by trying to be like anyone else.

How about that snowflake analogy? It's an oldie but a goodie. All snowflakes are unique, and God loves us more than snowflakes. You do the math. If He was so detailed with all the snowflakes, why the heck would He want any replicas when it came to His beloved children? I realize the irony of all this coming from a twin, but what might look like two replicas to those who first meet us is quite the opposite. God was no less creative when He knit the two of us together in our mother's womb. Our passions and talents are so different, and God is calling us to different things. Just remember, God loves you more than snowflakes. And in case you are second-guessing God's decision to use you, bite that tongue. God doesn't ask for put-together people. He wants real people who can admit their failings and point to God in the process.

In *Thirty One Days of Prayer for the Dreamer and the Doer*, Gina Zeidler shared a prayer about authenticity, and there was one line that I have mulled over for months. "We have cracks so that others can see you, Father." Those mistakes in my life, in your life, those things we want to cover up, they point to Christ because we all realize that He is the only way we have a chance of being whole. When I cover things up for fear of judgment, it's prideful. It's saying, "I want you to think I'm polished and pretty all on my own." Oh the freedom in knowing that letting our cracks show won't tarnish us but instead point to God!

Even as we read through a book on learning how to live a fruit-filled life, we must also understand we don't do this so people can see perfection in us. God bless if they *do* see where we fail along the way, because it reminds them that Christ is still working on me.

All those people you compare yourself to are battling the flesh right along with you, only we don't see that. We compare our whole and messy lives to the perfectly styled squares that someone has carefully curated to share with the world. It's not fair. Oh that's cute. You thought I meant, "It's not fair that they have it all together." Nope. I meant it's not fair that you compare the deepest parts of your soul to someone else's best in show.

You will reach someone that all those people you compare yourself to cannot. Don't be so focused on everyone else's audience that you can't even see your own audience. You have heard me say it, but I'll say it again: Satan doesn't have to get us to do bad things; he just has to keep us busy so we aren't doing good things. Is envy like busy? Is he putting people in front of us who have the very things we want just to distract us? Is it keeping us from realizing our potential?

Here are a few practical tips to rising above comparison:

1. Realize the effect comparison has on me. I don't think I truly understood what comparison did to me. I'm happy for my friends and don't envy them. But when I see a curated life of a "virtual friend" I don't see the struggles that came with the good. And it's those people I envy. They are far away though, so it comes in fleeting thoughts and I don't realize how much it disrupts my life. Proverbs 14:30 put things into perspective: "A heart at peace gives life to the body, but envy rots the bones." It seems so extreme of a picture, but how much does envy completely stop us from living a full life, one of gratitude and living a life of influence? How quickly do we get distracted from the one true purpose that God individually planned for *me*?

2. Realize the grass is not always greener. Stop watching someone else's tulips grow and start watering your own. How many times did you get what you thought would be better and it simply wasn't? Choose now to not see everyone else's story, talents, blessings as something you wish you had for yourself. It's coveting. You know, one of the 10 Commandments? Coveting changes our relationship with that person who has that thing we want. How can we love well when comparison and envy rule our thoughts when they are around?

3. Practice gratitude. Enough already, right? A grateful heart seems to be the cure-all remedy or, for my oily friends, the lavender.

Having a bad day? Dab a little gratitude on it. Tired of waiting on the Lord? Soak it in a mixture of hot water and gratitude. Feeling sad? Pop two gratitudes and drink a glass of water and call me in the morning. When we recognize where we really are and what God has really done in our life, we realize how silly we have been to be anything but grateful. Comparing ourselves to others tells God that He didn't get it right, that you should have a different set of skills or opportunities. Gratitude says, "Thank you, God. You know best."

4. Pray for God's direction. Oh and would you lookee here? The lovely Jenn Sprinkle wrote an amazing prayer on comparison in Thirty One Days of Prayer for the Dreamer and the Doer. If you weren't sure where to start, you do now. Here is a snippet:

Dear Lord, I pray that I would keep my eyes fixed on You and throw off all hindrances and distractions. I lay comparison at the foot of the Cross, asking You to replace this entanglement with a heart of celebration and obedience . . . Help me to see the areas of my online life that cause me to struggle with comparison and show me where I need to set boundaries and disconnect. Search me and see if there is any jealousy and envy in me and create in me a pure heart . . . Instill in me an unwavering confidence in my calling, gifts, and purpose to withstand the distraction of comparison from the enemy. Where I have wished for someone else's story, gifts, or success, replace it with a desire for the celebration of being a part of Your bigger plan and humbled at being used in even the smallest way.

HOMEWORK

WORK IT OUT

Grab your *Lessons from The Finishing School* workbook
or your worksheet, A GUIDE TO COMPARISON,
from the website and let the refining begin!

RECOMMENDED RESOURCES

*THIRTY ONE DAYS OF PRAYER FOR
THE DREAMER AND THE DOER*
book by jenn sprinkle and kelly rucker

Find links to the worksheet and extra resources at
VALMARIEPAPER.COM/HOMEWORK.
password: fairlady

21

Legends of the Hidden Temple

A GUIDE TO HEALTH

This body is broke, y'all. I hope the title wasn't too misleading. I do not in fact have this whole body thing figured out, but I am on a mission to learn.

I turned thirty recently, and I am feeling it. This week alone I feel like I have back pains, heart failure, and blood clots, to name a few. I also have hypochondria, but this was a pre-existing condition before I crossed into my thirties. So maybe it was only a hurt foot, stress related heart flutters, and sore muscles, but I don't want to see my body fall apart at the ripe old age of thirty. I should have at least a few more years.

I desire in my heart to be healthy and full of energy. If this book has shown me anything, it's that I've got a lot of living to do, and I want to be strong for it. Maybe you are like me, though, and you forget all the amazing things our bodies could do when we aren't taking care of them the way God intended. 2 Corinthians 7:1 says, "Therefore, since we have these promises, dear friends, let us purify ourselves from everything that contaminates body and spirit, perfecting holiness out of reverence for God." Instead, how many of us see our bodies not as perfecting holiness but as dilapidated and broke? Me. That's who. I just called my body broke like five seconds ago.

I do the same thing with foods. I forget that there are options that are not just "good for me" but that give me the energy I need, that help my muscles grow and make me feel better. I wish I could start seeing food as fuel instead of an opportunity for decadent delight.

I just started reading the book *Eat Move Sleep* by Tom Rath and am so fired up. Maybe the biggest thing we need to live a more healthy life is to simply have that idea in front of us more often. Health can be so easy to put on the back burner. It doesn't seem to affect anyone else, so in a world where people always need something from us, no one is championing the cause for our own health. That's our job, but we are too generous to think about ourselves, right? So many times we just respond to the loudest most dissonant sound in an effort to "make it stop," and unfortunately our aging body makes the quietest of these sounds.

Here's the thing we need to be empowered by. Cooperation. I loved how Rick Warren summed this idea up in *The Daniel Plan*. "We cannot achieve [lasting change and spiritual growth] on our own, but [God] will not do it without our cooperation. God supplies the resources and power for change, but we must make choices to activate those things in our lives."

That's all God is asking of us. He's got the resources to make it happen. Does this take some of the weight off you like it seems to do for me?

As I'm sure you know by now, one key to change is actually defining things. What does my life currently look like? What would I like my life to look like? I also like to look at past moments of victory to remind myself of what is possible. Unfortunately with my body, I have seen very little change. I simply haven't been able to make a good run at this whole healthy lifestyle. I come up with great ideas, but even then it normally ends with an idea. When Monday rolls around, because we all know a good healthy regimen starts on Monday, I have already forgotten what the plan was. Here's the thing. I feel like I have the info and know what to do, but I choose not to do it. I am weak-willed to my core when it comes to my health.

And really, I have some pretty convincing evidence that should have initiated some sort of change. I have a measuring stick that I see daily—my twin sister. At one point not too long ago, I was twenty pounds heavier than my sister. I'd love to blame it on Vivi, but I think I have to give some of the credit to the fact that I can't pass up a dessert, while Natalie can show incredible self-control and hits the gym while I hit the remote. It's a perfect case study. Twins with similar metabolism and genes and same starting weight. And there you have it. Exercise and good food choices win. Every time. Yet I still don't trust the system.

Maybe that's it? Maybe I need to remind myself to trust the system and trust what I have learned and the results I've seen in tons of others. When I go to the refrigerator and I see all the options, can I say to myself "trust the system" and be reminded that blueberries or cucumbers will benefit me more than raw cookie dough? When I want to sleep in or think my time would be better used working, could I simply say to myself "trust the system" and put my shoes on and head for the outdoors?

Even for those of you who have eaten healthy and seen little change, it might be hard to trust the system, but do we really think the alternative will help us more? It's easy to convince ourselves that it doesn't matter, but can you really deny the repercussions when you do slack off? We have to trust the system.

Oh, but the closet. The closet is where I lose the battle. Every. Single. Day. Clothes don't fit the way they fit six months ago when I was hitting the ballet barre three times a week. I normally leave my closet frustrated in either workout clothes (I use the term loosely), something terribly uncomfortable that bothers me all day, or one of the three outfits I have that make me feel great.

I know, I know. We should all love our bodies the way God made them, and I wholeheartedly agree with this. But at what point do we admit that the choices we keep making are turning the body God made into something He didn't intend? Can we stop slapping a "Jesus loves me just the way I am" sticker on my unhealthy habits and stop blaming genetics? Can we start appreciating the fact that Jesus does, in fact, love me no matter what and let that put a desire in me to cherish this body that was a gift from Him? Love is a feeling for sure, but it's also an action. Maybe we love our bodies by appreciating what God gave us (the feeling) and by taking care of it (the action).

Are we honoring God with the way we treat our bodies? I'm not talking to the girl who works out hard and still carries more weight than she'd like. I'm talking to the girl like me who has a dash of sass and ungratefulness that equals simply not giving a rip about what I should do to be a good steward of this body. If I love Him the way I say I do, does that not mean I would love my body the same in both the feeling and the action?

Romans 12:1 says, "Therefore, I urge you, brothers and sisters, in view of God's mercy, to offer your bodies as a living sacrifice, holy and pleasing to God—this is your true and proper worship."

My body is a sacrifice to the Lord. I can have the utmost awareness when it comes to my business that it is His to do with however He likes. If He wants me to produce this product or not that one, if He wants me to give more away, I am all ears. But my body? It seems so unusable for His kingdom. Perhaps this why I don't honor Him with my body like I will with my business. I simply don't see the potential of what He can do when I choose to be a good steward of it.

What can God do with a strong, healthy body? Just off the top of my head, I think about all those days I have spent sick because I neglected sleep and rest and ate junk. If I were strong and healthy, I could have spent more time serving and focused on others. When I get sick, I get cranky and self-focused, which is not exactly the recipe for being used for the kingdom of God. Certainly God uses sickness every day to bring glory to Himself, but this is not my signal to give up.

So what does it mean to be used by God daily and through this body? This makes me think about the Israelites and how God gave them just enough food for each day. Referring to the manna, Exodus 16:19 says, "Let no one leave any of it over till the morning."

God provided nourishment for the day. They were to use it fully every day. We should live boldly each day for the Lord, not hoarding energy as if God won't provide for the next day. I rationalize this to myself often. I need to take a break for thirty minutes before I get tired, so I don't get tired. The truth is, if I work out or get moving, I could build my stamina to where thirty-minute breaks on the couch aren't a necessity, because I have energy for life. I can't help but think this is how God fuels our body by giving us enough energy for each day for us to use up completely.

Sometimes our lack is not from giving too much away but clinging too much or hoarding it. I need to trust that God will provide. I think I need to hear that again. Sometimes our lack is not from giving too much away but clinging too much or hoarding it. Lord, let that truth wash over us.

Isaiah 40:31 (ESV) promises, "But they who wait for the Lord shall renew their strength; they shall mount up with wings like eagles; they shall run and not be weary; they shall walk and not faint."

Want to know why people love shows like *The Biggest Loser*? Because it gives us hope that what we thought was impossible is possible. For the contestants, they are overcome by confidence as their once feeble bodies move like they never have before. God is the answer to this in our lives. He is our strength, and we must only cooperate and tap into His resources. What does cooperating look like in your life? In what ways have you been stiff-necked? And how does God's presence and power change everything?

Here are a few lies that we have to reject:

1. It doesn't work. Yes, healthy foods and exercise do work. And even if they aren't helping shed the pounds, donuts and ice cream sure aren't the answer.

2. This will satisfy. Overindulging rarely satisfies past that last bite, and actually most of the time we stop enjoying it even before we finish.

3. I deserve it. This is our selfish flesh talking that says we are entitled to things. You know what you deserve? Energy, focus and a strong body.

4. I have to take care of others. Yes, you probably do, but you can do that so much better when you are full of energy and not burnt out.

Philippians 2:13 (NLT) says, "For God is working in you, giving you the desire and the power to do what pleases him." Don't think for a second that you are doing this alone in your own strength. If that were the case, I'd be a lost cause. Instead, dwell on this promise and ask the Lord for the desire to honor Him with your body.

H O M E W O R K

WORK IT OUT

Grab your *Lessons from The Finishing School* workbook
or your worksheet, A GUIDE TO HEALTH,
from the website and let the refining begin!

RECOMMENDED RESOURCES

EAT MOVE SLEEP
book by tom rath

EAT PRETTY
book by jolene hart

Find links to the worksheet and extra resources at
VALMARIEPAPER . COM / HOMEWORK.
password: fairlady

22

The Best Rule Ever

A GUIDE TO REST

When we were at camp one summer, we would have what they called a Solo. It was three hours alone with God. THREE HOURS, PEOPLE! I was a teenager with the spiritual attention span of a worship song, maybe two. If texting had been around, you'd better believe I would have been texting my friend "WTHATFR?" In layman's terms, "What the heck? Are they for real?" All we had with us was our Bible, a journal, and the leaflet titled "My Heart—Christ's Home." Oh, and God's beautiful green earth, the lush mountains, and views of Colorado. So as you can see, our counselors were clearly trying to torture us.

When I came out on the other side, I was a better person for it. I loved it and decided I'd have to do this again. I sit here fourteen years later realizing I never did it. Was I only kidding myself? Was it not really that refreshing/life-changing? I don't think so. I think it was; I just got caught up going around the merry-go-round of life and couldn't figure out where to step off.

The idea of the Sabbath seems a little old fashioned to me. We are living in the twenty-first century. The Sabbath was "invented" before all our distractions. I can't unplug or slow this train I call a mind down. There is just too much going on. That, my friend, is why it is more important than ever that we do slow down and rest. Whether it's on the actual Sabbath or not isn't the most important thing, but pick a day during the week to truly rest. I think this is one of the hardest lessons we can learn in today's society. Rest is not valued nearly as much as busy is.

What does it mean to truly rest and to keep the Sabbath anyway? If you are the cheating kind, here are the cliff notes of this chapter: I like to think of rest as a reset from the world—a chance to hibernate for a short period of time and wash away the world's definition of everything and get God-centered again. We manage to get a bit off kilter or maybe our glasses start to get a rosy tint. What if we even thought of it like a bath? We are washing away the world's expectations, our own faulty thinking, and our anxieties about work. We are instead soaking in God's presence, His truth, and His joy. And giving these things our undivided attention. In *Sacred Rhythms* by Ruth Haley Barton, she calls the Sabbath a day "set apart, devoted completely to rest, worship and delighting in God." Delighting in God. I love that. I want that.

Remember how we talked about the Lord's provision of manna to the Hebrews in Exodus? They're baaaaack. Those poor naive Hebrews can't do anything right.

Each morning everyone gathered as much as they needed, and when the sun grew hot, it melted away. On the sixth day, they gathered twice as much—two omers for each person—and the leaders of the community came and reported this to Moses. He said to them, "This is what the Lord commanded: 'Tomorrow is to be a day of sabbath rest, a holy sabbath to the Lord. So bake what you want to bake and boil what you want to boil. Save whatever is left and keep it until morning.'" So they saved it until morning, as Moses commanded, and it did not stink or get maggots in it. "Eat it today," Moses said, "because today is a sabbath to the Lord. You will not find any of it on the ground today. Six days you are to gather it, but on the seventh day, the Sabbath, there will not be any." Nevertheless, some of the people went out on the seventh day to gather it, but they found none. Then the Lord said to Moses, "How long will you refuse to keep my commands and my instructions? Bear in mind that the Lord has given you the Sabbath; that is why on the sixth day he gives you bread for two days. Everyone is to stay where they are on the seventh day; no one is to go out." So the people rested on the seventh day. - Exodus 16:21-30

I'm just over here straightening out my dress and thumbing my nose at all the murderers, thieves, and sinners, completely ignoring the fact that my not observing the Sabbath is disobedience. Y'all caught that, right? He's not suggesting it; He is commanding it. And just like that, I've steamrolled so many opportunities, nay commands, over the years to keep the Sabbath. Let's call a spade a spade, won't we? Why must I insist on watering down His Word to something that's easier to hear? I digress.

We've got the flesh telling us rest doesn't matter. We've got the flesh saying we have way too much to do and that our time would be better spent playing catchup. We've got the flesh dropping hints for a thousand different things that would matter more. We've got the flesh telling us it's simply not practical to "waste" the time. Dear friends, it is no waste of time. But we can't help but believe this lie, so we turn the Sabbath into another day for progress. Y'all know my love for efficiency. This concept is one of the most elusive for me to grasp. Wouldn't more time working equal more things done? And for His kingdom, no less. Okay, my kingdom, but I almost had you convinced I wasn't selfish, right?

In my limited Sabbath experience, I have seen how hard it is to slow down my mind and get out of the get-it-done mode. How many times on a Sabbath do you find yourself feeling like there are not enough hours in the day to accomplish all you want to accomplish? Maybe instead of giving those things more time, we need to step back and simply give God our days. God's math is always better than mine, and I don't just mean because I'm terrible at math. I mean because He can multiply and divide time the same way He multiplied manna for another day. My humble mind tends to get stuck on days one through six. I know what to expect as far as portions, and this is what I expect from day seven, forgetting that God is not limited by measures. If He wants to dole out a double portion one day of the week, He is more than capable. I'm like a child who needs consistent reinforcement of the rules. I keep catching myself in moments where I have to remind myself that the Sabbath is not about progress. It's about rest. And I'm starting to get it. Now if only I got a cupcake every time, I think the positive reinforcement of this idea of rest would seal the deal. Did I say cupcake? I meant carrot.

As if His provision wasn't enough, the passage said the manna did not stink or get maggots. That was God's protection of it. This tells me that He is cheering us on and providing His best for us, giving us all the hope of enjoying it, including non-stinky or maggoty manna.

Here is the kicker: we have to plan for it. I love what Jen Hatmaker says about Exodus 16 in her book 7. I know, this chick again, Valerie? Just go buy her book already. It's brilliant.

Originally, the Sabbath had to be planned for, food gathered a day in advance. It wasn't handed to the Hebrews on a silver platter. This principle remains. I still have to plan for the Sabbath, tying up loose ends and gathering what we'll need. I still have to prepare the family for rest, enforcing healthy boundaries and protecting our calendar. I still have to set work aside and trust in the wisdom of God's design. "Bear in mind that the Lord has given you the Sabbath."

I never even thought about the fact that the reason I don't enjoy a true day of rest is not because God doesn't provide it but because I don't prepare practically and spiritually for it. I do nothing to protect what He does give. For the Hebrews, that meant baking and boiling. For you that may mean grocery shopping, finishing emails the day before, and quieting your mind early in the morning to prepare for the day. It's currently Saturday night, and I was hoping with all hope that I could "Sabbath" tomorrow. Can we make that a verb? Anyways, while I was hoping, I wasn't planning. The cupboards are bare, and I have a little girl who eats more than I do, and as you already learned, I'm not a dainty eater.

Next week, Sabbath? You. Are. Mine. Oh and by that I mean you are God's. I will be planning for it, and I will remember that if I don't plan for it, it won't happen. I can look back on the last gazillion Sundays as my example. For our family, I'm envisioning a Saturday morning spent on chores and errands and afternoon of adventure to prepare for our day of rest. Update: That next Saturday was filled with yard work, garden planting, groceries, and laundry. We fell into bed feeling like we conquered that day and breathed a sweet sigh of relief that when we woke, it would be Sabbath. The day was a complete delight and has me wanting more Sundays just like it.

This whole one-day-a-week thing shouldn't be that big of deal. Here is the God of the universe who gives gifts of grace, love, and provision for me to experience any life worth living and all He asks for is one day a week. It could be reversed and we could have six Sabbath days a week and one day to work, and we could still not justify hemming and hawing at how we deserved more days. But we are talking one day a week! When I look at the reality of that, I feel silly that I make it seem so difficult to do. Get over yourself, Valerie. The world will not end if you don't go to the grocery store or tidy everything for the new week. Rest. Rest. I'm taking public speaking cues from Jesus who, when He repeated something, He meant it. Rest. Rest. I even feel myself slow down as I hear those words repeated in my head. Rest. Rest. I am liking the sound of this. Rest. Rest.

On this one day a week, can we reverse our minds and know that the more we try to do, the less we will reap? Can we reverse our minds and know that there is huge abundance in the stillness? Can we actually rest in Matthew 11:28-30? "Come to me, all you who are weary and burdened, and I will give you rest. Take my yoke upon you and learn from me, for I am gentle and humble in heart, and you will find rest for your souls. For my yoke is easy and my burden is light."

Why is this called a chapter on rest and not just the Sabbath? Because we need rest in other ways; but I think this lesson of the Sabbath, if we can learn it well, will teach us all we need to know about rest as a whole. If we can't understand God's biblical design for rest as it pertains to the Sabbath, how can we fully understand rest at all? Start practicing rest once a week and ask God to reveal more truths about where else you need pockets of rest.

How do we practically do this? I'm still new to this whole Sabbath thing, so I don't have much advice, but I can tell you a few basic tips to practice.

1. Take a break from technology. Our phones, computers, and TV don't equal true rest. And given that the idea of the Sabbath is to spend time with the Lord and delighting in Him, unless you are watching *Passion of the Christ* on Netflix, following Paul on Instagram, or reading the Bible online, technology will only create another obstacle to rest. I'm so guilty of looking to technology for my rest, but Psalm 62:1 says, "My soul finds rest in God alone." There is no room for interpretation on that one fellow scholars. Extra points for succinctness on that one, David.

2. Take a break from work. This one we are most familiar with. It's probably what you envision as keeping the Sabbath. This might be easy for the fry cook at Chick-Fil-A but not so much for the person with email on their phone, the teacher who needs to grade papers, or the work-at-home mom.

3. Take a break from spending. This does two things. If we are spending money, someone is bound to be working because of it, thus perpetuating the working on Sunday mentality. Consuming also keeps us focused on worldly things. If you are buying Bibles for poor kids in Peru, by all means ignore me, but hitting up the J. Crew because you aren't working and you've got some free time isn't exactly what God had in mind. I went to college in a small town, and lots of places were closed on Sunday. This was annoying sometimes, but I learned to love the quietness of a whole town that you could come to expect like clockwork every week. Imagine if we all retreated to our homes—family and friends invited, of course—for one day a week.

4. Have a mind that is set on joy in the Lord. My first

Sabbath was so sweet, y'all. It was peaceful and slow. My mind was different. I took a nap, and I smiled even when I didn't know why I was smiling. But I also did some laundry and cleaned the kitchen. And even these things I was able to do with a different mentality. Let's not turn into the Pharisees who seemed to turn everything into a mindless rule. It's about the posture of our hearts as we do things. If we are honest with ourselves, we know the things that equal rest in the Father and those things that don't.

5. Plan for it. Without planning, something will try to yank you out of your happy place. It's inevitable. Plan for what you can or don't be surprised when you have a thousand things to do before Monday and Sunday morning has rolled around.

6. Set the environment. Put distractions away like the computer or the remote. Pull out the Bibles, books, blankets, candles, and anything else that signals a slower mindset for your family. Oily friends, we love to diffuse frankincense on Sundays to signal a different focus for the day.

Tah-tah-taht. Shh. Shh. Don't fight it. No excuses. Just try it. Juuuuust try it. Trust me, you are going to like this. That's something you don't hear with every command, but let's give it up for the big man upstairs for being so generous. Sink into your most comfortable chair or sweats, grab a cup of tea, and cozy up to what Ruth has to say in Sacred Rhythms about what we can expect once we experience the Sabbath.

> You will long to wake up to a day that stretches out in front of you with nothing in it but rest and delight. You will long for a simple way to turn your heart toward God in worship without much effort. You will long for a space

in time when the pace is slow and family and friends linger with one another, savoring one another's presence because no one has anywhere else to go. You will long to sit on your own couch or on your own deck because it is yours, a gift from God that often gets overlooked in the rush of things. You will long for the day when you can crawl back into bed for an afternoon nap, which is all the more delicious because on this day you know that you are doing exactly what God wants you to do . . . You will long to read a book for pleasure . . . You will long for a rhythm of working and resting that you can count on.

How beautiful does this sound? Is this really what I'm fighting against experiencing once a week? It sounds like a heavenly vacation. And to think God commands us to delight in Him in this way? We are blessed indeed, believers. Best rule ever.

HOMEWORK

WORK IT OUT

Grab your *Lessons from The Finishing School* workbook
or your worksheet, A GUIDE TO REST,
from the website and let the refining begin!

RECOMMENDED RESOURCES

THE REST OF GOD
book by mark buchanan

Find links to the worksheet and extra resources at
VALMARIEPAPER.COM/HOMEWORK.
password: fairlady

23

The Space Between

A GUIDE TO MARGIN

Besides the obvious, the Bible, there have been few books that have changed my life as much the book *Margin* by Richard Swenson. I remember being a few pages in and immediately had to grab a notebook because it provoked so many more thoughts and ideas I didn't want to forget learning.

Margin is the space between our load and our limits. So many of us live maxed out, and when extra is thrown our way, we break. Richard says, "The spontaneous tendency of our culture is to inexorably add detail to our lives: one more option, one more commitment, one more expectation, one more purchase, one more debt, one more change, one more job, one more decision." We are hell bent on more being better, and that's not the vision God has for us.

If His Son is any indication to us of what the Father intended for us (and it is!), it's not over scheduling and saying yes to everything. Jesus didn't heal every single sick person, though He could have. Jesus didn't preach or pour into people every second of the day. He stole away by Himself or with the disciples for moments of rest and being renewed by God.

Margin is incredibly biblical, though the term is nowhere in the Word. If our lives are so overcrowded with the things that we fill it up with, we leave no white space for God to work. Do we make ourselves available to be used by God? Are we a vessel waiting to be filled? Or did we hit maximum capacity a year ago?

Richard puts it this way: "His asking us to walk the second mile, to carry others' burdens, to witness to the Truth at any opportunity, and to teach our children when we sit, walk, lie, and stand all presuppose we have margin and that we make it available for His purposes. Obedience to these commands is often not schedulable."

The greatest moments in our life will probably be things that never make it into our calendar. Doesn't it make sense that if that calendar is full, we will miss out on so much?

Our world is little help when it comes to living with margin. Our culture has accepted busy as the high status of choice. Busy has somehow translated to a successful life, while a life with room to breathe translates to missing out on something. But I want a life that doesn't just fit the world's definition of good. We can't do everything, and I honestly don't even want to do everything even if I could. We have to redefine what a "successful" life looks like. I jotted down what margin meant to me.

"The life I desire is unbusy. It's filled with the people that matter, work I'm passionate about and plenty of room to serve others. It's free from over-filled closets, over-flowing toy chests, unkept cars, piled high refrigerators or sinks, crowded cabinets and racks. It's not controlled by the stuff that surrounds me, half of which I could care less about a week after it is acquired. Instead it is led by the Holy Spirit, free to roam about my day to lead me into heavenly-ordained appointments where God is glorified. Where refreshment happens with a hot bath or hot tea and a good book instead of in front of a screen. Where conversations are filled with a few less words and far more listening. Where whispers from the Lord are heard clearly because all the noise and chatter no longer reigns. Where peace is the overwhelming emotion instead of heart-racing anxiety. Where joy is the choice. Where less is more."

This is my definition of margin, and this is the life I desired even with a four-month-old baby in tow at the time. I wrote that on February 26, 2014, and a year later I am experiencing it. God poured out so much grace in this area on me and allowed me to have a life of margin. If it hasn't been clear by the number of books I've read or worksheets I have designed, I am goal-oriented, but this idea of margin and living for more than progress has been surprisingly enticing to me.

I had a friend tell me she didn't know how I do it all. I told her that's because I don't, in the least sassy way possible, I promise. Here's a short list of things I don't do: I don't go to every birthday party or shower. I don't watch a ton of TV (anymore!). I don't have more than one night of the week with an ongoing commitment. I don't say yes to every interview or blog feature. And for things I do a lot, I have a system to simplify the process as much as possible. I have spent too much time believing that a full life meant a full schedule, house, or closet. I'm here to tell you, it's not. And this, my friends, is your chapter to breathe and to know that those things that matter most to living your life for God can happen without turning your world into a fury of a more packed schedule.

I documented as I tried to make this idea of living with margin. There are some moments of victory, but mostly those moments where it all fell apart during the journey. I hope it will inspire your own journey to find a life with more white space and room for God to roam. But I want you to think about something as you read.

Do you really want this? My husband and I always talk about this. If you want something, you will work hard for it. If it's not really important to you, you won't do it. You will keep saying yes to things that don't matter to you. You will give your time away to anyone who asks. You could make a million excuses for why this won't work for you. I always get annoyed with the "mom game." You know when we all try to one-up each other with whose life is more disgusting or exhausting. That's a game I stopped wanting to win a long time ago. This whole margin talk can bring out that same competitive spirit. Your husband works eighty hours a week. You don't have money to say no to things. You have too many friends. Now you're just bragging. But really, this is the fork in the road for a lot of people, and excuses are the difference between people who find margin and people who keep their overloaded calendars and closets because they don't think they can change things.

Here's a hard truth. Busyness doesn't just happen to us. We choose it. Do you hate me for saying that? Are you squirming a bit now? Don't worry. Me too. I read this incredible quote from an article by Professor Bruce Hindmarsh called "You Have Just Enough Time." You might want to buckle up. "Busyness is moral laziness [because it is often a statement of our self-importance and our excuse to be inattentive to people]. . . . But God has given us just enough time to do what we need to do moment by moment to respond to him. And his grace is there; it is eternally present. Every moment is a sacrament where time touches eternity and there is exactly enough time to do what God has called us to do."

Busyness is our answer for not making tough, moral decisions about where our time should go. Some decisions are uncomfortable to make, so we choose to just do it instead of making a tough call. It's laziness. And the truth is, God gave us the time we need. Does our complaining of being too busy slap God in the face like my comments that I'm not pretty enough or smart enough do?

If you are okay with letting the excuses decide this for you, you are welcome to, but if you are ready to quit justifying why this wouldn't work for you, I'm cheering you on, and I hope my journey will spur on your own quest for margin.

March 3, 2014

The margin God is placing in my life is truly amazing. Having time to cook for our friends during their busy season will be used by God. Had I been running around frantically, I would have never volunteered. This slower pace makes sense to me. I hope I don't forget this feeling.

March 7, 2014

Right now as we talk about house plans, I am consumed with the thought of keeping it simple. I want a house that doesn't inspire envy but instead inspires peace and joy and even contentment with what they have. I want furniture and things that don't keep my attention when guests are there but instead on people.

March 18, 2014

I have found myself overwhelmed by the shortness of the evenings lately. And Vivi taking shorter naps has made for crazier days, which make the relaxing nights that much more needed. I'm trying to ask myself what work things I can get off my plate. And to also remind myself that the less I plan for the evenings, the more enjoyable they are. The key for them not turning into TV and FB nights is simply to think more intentionally. Trying to remind myself of the amazing way I feel experiencing more margin in my life. Hoping it will keep me focused to make great choices.

March 21, 2014

God is good. In the midst of a crazy week, I am slowing down, putting the phone away, and enjoying Vivi. I feel like I've been able to appreciate her in a whole new way. And I am seeing things I never noticed about her as she grows. Being able to feel peace despite an empty, crossed-off to-do list feels so good because I won't be able to control some busy seasons. I love my life and I'm so glad I can say that even when everything is not perfect.

March 24, 2014

There is just too much stuff. It drives me bonkers. I spend an insane amount of time picking up things and truthfully, it's probably not as insane as other houses. Everything feels a bit too big to chew, though. I want to remind myself to take small steps. A little bit each night. I don't have to bite it all at once.

March 31, 2014

A wardrobe of margin. I think what makes it possible is living contented and knowing I'm not trying to never wear the same thing twice. I am perfectly okay if someone sees me in the same thing over and over again. They don't care. Why do I project on them that they do care? It's so silly.

April 2, 2014

My quest for margin continues. It's 5 o'clock in the afternoon and I'm sitting in my comfy chair writing and reading. I can choose this. Most days I don't and instead think checking one more thing off my list is what will make me happy. It doesn't. Yet somehow I forget that every day. Progress becomes my enemy instead of my friend when I see it as my source of joy. I long for refreshment each evening in prepping for the next day, Pinterest, and TV. Not tonight!

April 23, 2014

Stop striving for me. It makes life exhausting to always need to be getting enough work time or more time to read or more time for chores. Live life. And enjoy it. It's the oldest lesson ever. See the glass as half full. Don't beat myself up or stress myself out because I only got to read for 15 minutes. See that as a victory. Be grateful for the rest I do have.

May 7, 2014

My evening after Vivi goes down have included my Bible and book reading. That has been the extent of my margin. What's holding me back? What's keeping me in the cycle of chaos? Seriously write them down:

- I'm not praying
- I'm using social media too much
- Dealing with my lost wallet stuff still
- So many orders, not enough supplies
- Not using my time sheets
- Craving crappy foods

Are there things I can do to get rid of these issues?

May 15, 2014

There is such a fine line between productivity and striving too hard. Life is just busy right now. I'm trying to produce a shoot/new collection. Yesterday at the coffee shop, I buckled down and got a lot of the things on my list done in a short amount of time. I psyched myself up and could do it. Normally, I think I just meander through my list with no real sense of urgency. Without realizing that working a little smarter means I can work a little less.

August 18, 2014

I am so out of sorts right now. I feel like things are spilling out of my life and there is clearly no margin. I want to do it all. I want the house to be perfect. I want to do a ton of products for Tinsel & Treasures and I want them all in time for our photo shoot. People stress me out rather than me serving them joyfully. Show me, Lord, what things don't line up with my core mission:

- Stressing or buying more for the shoot
- Blogging unless it's my heart
- Distractions like Instagram
- Junk food that leaves me distracted
- TV during work days
- No preparing for next day
- Pretending (the song and dance of what is expected from Val of Val Marie Paper)
- Waste and excess (going to lunch when we have food, not making a real lunch but getting up four times for snacks, too many clothes and too many things)
- Working from the couch or recliner
- Not having true rest

I think all my journaling is what really helped this idea to stick. It was in my head for months. It's part of the reason you find a worksheet at the end of each chapter so you can work it out and not just close your book and forget about it. And it's why my best suggestion to you to experience margin is to keep a journal of your own as you go through this process:

1. Journal in moments you enjoy margin, and journal in moments you miss it completely.
2. See what you did to make either happen.
3. Make more things happen in those moments you experience margin.

Here are a few areas we can have margin in our life, and you are actually already familiar with them:

1. Schedule - This is the big one. Our chapter on boundaries talked about how to figure out how to say no and yes to things. Remember, it is a choice to be busy no matter how much we think otherwise. God created time and knew what He was doing. Trust Him and start chopping.

2. Stuff - I am giggling as I sit here in a pile of papers and notes and books to make sure I'm not missing a single thing to include in the book. I am going through pages and secretly hoping there is nothing important on them so the stack I can toss is greater than the stack currently on my bed. You heard me preach enough about the stuff in the chapter on minimalism, but just in case you forgot already, get rid of some things.

3. Brain Space - There is no lack of ideas or information today. Just hop on Pinterest or Facebook. We've got to cut out some of the noise, not all of it, but some. That might mean you stop pinning ideas you will never ever in a million years make time for. We fantasize about a day when we will have time for all this stuff, but the real question is, even when I do find margin in my life, will I want to fill it up with that? The chapter on contentment focused on this idea of not needing more things to be happy but being happy with what we've got.

4. Progress - What's that mean? Margin in our progress? Margin and progress are in a tug of war. Margin tells me to take a few moments to relax and refresh when I'm busy. Progress tells me to check something off. Progress in itself is not a bad idea. We should be moving forward and growing. But I can't let it consume my world. If

I'm not crossing something off my list, I feel like I just wasted time. This, my friends, is why we find ourselves burnt out and exhausted. Our free time isn't truly free. We jam pack it full of things that aren't needed. For some reason, we think that we have a finite list of things to do and once we are completely done, we will rest. Our chapter on rest will hopefully inspire you to slow down.

My journey is far from over, but I am grateful for where God has taken me. I saved this chapter for last because so many of the things discussed already will help you live a life of margin. This is where it all comes together.

When life is too busy, we neglect friendships, we go through drive-thrus for dinner, we skip our quiet times, and forget about serving. Does that sound fulfilling or satisfying to you? It sure isn't my definition.

Want to know the most fertile conditions for cultivating a prayer life or spending time in the Word? Or finding balance or growing friendships? Want to know the most fertile conditions for releasing creativity or showing hospitality? Or making God-centered goals? It's having space and time that allows us to be intentional. You are far more capable than you may realize to experience true transformation in your life. Give God room to roam and tap into His resource.

HOMEWORK

WORK IT OUT

Grab your *Lessons from The Finishing School* workbook
or your worksheet, A GUIDE TO MARGIN,
from the website and let the refining begin!

RECOMMENDED RESOURCES

MARGIN
book by richard swenson

Find links to the worksheet and extra resources at
VALMARIEPAPER. COM/HOMEWORK.
password: fairlady

24

See You at the Reunion

A GUIDE TO GRADUATION

It's for your own good. It's for your own good. It's for your own good. These words kept pummeling me during one of Vivi's and my walks. I thought about creating habits, resting, minimalism, forgiveness, self-control. All of it. Everything I learned. As I thought about one more failure in my pursuit of contentment and my impending desire to give up, I realized it was all worth it.

All those lessons I had learned were for my own good. For so long I had seen God trying to discipline me as punishments and fun-suckers or torture that God used to make me holy, but the very result of all those things brought my own life beauty and meaning.

When we fritter our days away on worthless things, Satan smiles. But when we pursue holiness, both the failures and the victories point to God.

When broken people see other broken people pray faithfully and hear from God, God gets the glory.

When broken people see other broken people spend time in the Word consistently despite a crazy to-do list, God gets the glory.

When broken people see other broken people make goals not simply for their own gain, God gets the glory.

When broken people see other broken people ignore distractions and follow God faithfully, God gets the glory.

When broken people see other broken people exercise self-control, God gets the glory.

When broken people see other broken people overcome bad habits, God gets the glory.

When broken people see other broken people create boundaries that protect their priorities, God gets the glory.

When broken people see other broken people experience a life free from chaos, God gets the glory.

When broken people see other broken people live a simple life, God gets the glory.

When broken people see other broken people enjoy real, life-giving friendships, God gets the glory.

When broken people see other broken people put effort into serving others well, God gets the glory.

When broken people see other broken people wait patiently for God's plan, God gets the glory.

When broken people see other broken people experience joy despite their circumstances, God gets the glory.

When broken people see other broken people live with contentment not dependent on things, God gets the glory.

When broken people see other broken people make a difference to others, God gets the glory.

When broken people see other broken people forgive instead of stay bitter, God gets the glory.

When broken people see other broken people bring awareness and hope to the issues in our world, God gets the glory.

When broken people see other broken people experience peace despite temptation to fear, God gets the glory.

When broken people see other broken people support their peers instead of compare, God gets the glory.

When broken people see other broken people treat their bodies as God's temple, God gets the glory.

When broken people see other broken people spend their Sabbath delighting in God, God gets the glory.

When broken people see other broken people create white space and margin for God to work, God gets the glory.

These things simply cannot happen apart from the Lord. And y'all, when we see God do all these things in our life, we are changed.

The refining process is messy. You will have plenty of setbacks as you run the race set before you. Don't see them as failures and don't hide them. Our flaws point to Jesus. Our victories and growth point to Him too. When someone can see a truly transformed person who was in no way capable of changing on their own, those onlookers are compelled to embrace the truth that there is a power way bigger than us.

We are being refined by one magnificent God.

This session of *The Finishing School* is coming to an end. It's time I toss you out into society and reveal the refinement that's happening in your life.

Everyone says they will stay connected after graduation, but can that please be true for us? Connect on Instagram @ValMariePaper for daily inspiration. I would love to keep encouraging you as you walk through this journey to living the life you love. And drop an email and share what you have learned and how this book as helped you grow. I could use the encouragement too!

ACKNOWLEDGMENTS

To my husband Tyler, thank you for believing in me. I don't say that lightly. When I let doubt creep in that this book wasn't worth writing, you believed in it. Making you proud is something that has energized me throughout this process.

To my sister Natalie, thank you for your never ending time and support. I feel part of this book belongs to you as you helped shape it so much. I'd be a lost goose without you.

To Lorien, the big sister I never had, thank you for being the first to read a choppy manuscript. You gave me direction and more importantly, so much support and encouragement to make this book happen. You are one of my biggest cheerleaders and I am forever grateful.

To my pastor Mr. Dennis Malcolm, thank you for leading Trinity Bible Church so well and teaching me so much over the past 20 years. Thank you for taking the time to read The Finishing School to make sure it was according to God's truth.

To Mae and Ashley, thank you for your constant enthusiasm and support. You girls have lifted me up so much and I hope I can return the favor one day!

To Gretchen, thank you for letting the Lord speak through you so many times throughout the writing and editing process. You have been such an encouragement to me.

To Miss Duke, my creative writing teacher. You cultivated in me a love for books and writing that I could have never imagined what it would inspire 12 years later.

To my parents, thank you for setting my feet on this narrow path. You always say we are better than y'all raised us, but if that's true, it's only because y'all gave God the reins.

NOTES

CHAPTER 2: WORRIER TO WARRIOR
Timothy Keller, *Prayer* (New York, Penguin Group, 2014)
Jennifer White, *Prayers for the New Bride* (Green Forest, New Leaf Press, 2015)

CHAPTER 3: THE GOOD GOOD BOOK
Jen Hatmaker, *7* (Nashville, B&H Publishing Group, 2012)
Jen Wilkin, *Women in the Word* (Wheaton, Crossway, 2014)
Fred Craddock, The Collected Sermons of Fred B. Craddock (Louisville, Westminster John Knox Press, 2011)
Shelene Bryan, *Love, Skip, Jump* (Nashville, Nelson Books, 2014)
Dictionary.com, "potency," dictionary.reference.com/browse/potency

CHAPTER 4: GOAL #2: BE WEIRD
John C. Maxwell, *Today Matters* (New York, Time Warner Book Group, 2004)

CHAPTER 5: WHAT I GAVE UP FOR LENT
Laura Vanderkam, *168 Hours* (New York, Penguin Group, 2010)

CHAPTER 6: HALF A BAG OF POWDERED DONUTS
Dictionary.com, "steadfast." dictionary.reference.com/browse/steadfast
David Mathis, "Self-Control and the Power of Christ." desiringgod.org/

articles/self-control-and-the-power-of-christ

Edward Welch, "Self-Control: The Battle Against One More." The Journal of Biblical Counseling, Volume 19, Number 2, Winter 2001 gospelspirituality.files.wordpress.com/2012/01/self-control-the-battle-against-22one-more22-by-ed-welch.pdf

CHAPTER 7: CUE THE CHOCOLATE

Jack D. Hodges, *The Power of Habit* (Bloomington, 1stBooks, 2003)

Charles Duhigg, *The Power of Habit* (New York, Random House, 2014)

Darren Hardy, *The Compound Effect* (Boston, First Capo Press, 2013)

Shawn Achor, *The Happiness Advantage* (New York, Crown Publishing, 2010)

CHAPTER 8: BLOOD IS THICKER THAN PAPER

Richard Swenson, *Margin* (Colorado Springs, NavPress, 2004)

Lin Yutang, *The Importance of Living* (New York, William Morrow and Company, Inc, 1965)

Shelene Bryan, *Love, Skip, Jump* (Nashville, Nelson Books, 2014)

CHAPTER 11: BRUNETTES AND CIVICS

Donald Miller, *Scary Close* (Nashville, Thomas Nelson, 2014)

CHAPTER 12: STUPID ICE CREAM

Shauna Niequist, October 2014 twitter.com/sniequist/status/52746 8643794554880

Shauna Niequist, *Bread & Wine* (Grand Rapids, Zondervan, 2013)

Zoe Nathan, "A Perfectly Imperfect Hostess." October 2014, http://darlingmagazine.org/perfectly-imperfect-hostess/

CHAPTER 13: NEVER BEEN KISSED

Natalie Metrejean, *Wholeheartedly* (Lafayette, 2015)

CHAPTER 14: HARRY POTTER DOES BROADWAY

Ann Voskamp, *One Thousand Gifts* (Grand Rapids, Zondervan, 2010)

CHAPTER 16: I HEART TECH
Shelene Bryan, *Love, Skip, Jump* (Nashville, Nelson Books, 2014)
Jenni Catron, *Clout* (Nashville, Nelson Books, 2014)

CHAPTER 17: SERMON HALL PASS
Lysa Terkeurst, *Unglued* (Grand Rapids, Zondervan, 2012)

CHAPTER 18: BURIED IN THE SAND
Ann Voskamp, *One Thousand Gifts* (Grand Rapids, Zondervan, 2010)
Susan Jeffers, *Feel the Fear and Do it Anyway* (Toronto, Fawcett Books, 1987)

CHAPTER 20: YOU, ME, AND THE OTHER GAL
Jen Hatmaker, *7* (Nashville, B&H Publishing Group, 2012)
Gina Zeidler, *31 Days of Prayer for the Dreamer and the Doer* (Fort Worth, NyreePress Literary Group, 2014)
Jenn Sprinkle, *31 Days of Prayer for the Dreamer and the Doer* (Fort Worth, NyreePress Literary Group, 2014)

CHAPTER 21: LEGENDS OF THE HIDDEN TEMPLE
Rick Warren, *The Daniel Plan* (Grand Rapids, Zondervan, 2013)
Tom Rath, *Eat Move Sleep* (Arlington, Missionday, 2013)

CHAPTER 22: THE BEST RULE EVER
Ruth Haley Barton, *Sacred Rhythms* (Downers Grove, InterVarsity Press, 2006)
Jen Hatmaker, *7* (Nashville, B&H Publishing Group, 2012)

CHAPTER 23: THE SPACE BETWEEN
Richard Swenson, *Margin* (Colorado Springs, NavPress, 2004)
Prof. Bruce Hindmarsh, "You Have Just Enough Time." April 2014, desiringgod.org/articles/you-have-just-enough-time

THE FINISHING SCHOOL COLLECTION

LESSONS FROM TFS WORKBOOK

Work out what you learned in The Finishing School in this companion guide by answering questions, jotting down things you want to remember, action steps to put things in motion and a prayer for each area discussed in the book.

"A GUIDE TO" JOURNAL

Grab our lined journal (or two!) and chronicle your goals, victories and failures for growth in a particular area of life. It also makes a sweet keepsake of how far you have come on your journey!

TFS FLASH CARD

The set includes 22 cards, one for each of the lessons from the book. Write down quotes from The Finishing School or other books and resources on each topic that you want to remember.

THE EVERYDAY COLLECTION

WOMEN'S PRAYER JOURNAL

Organized 6-month journal with prompts and sections to fill out before the 1st, then pray throughout the month.

GRATITUDE JOURNAL

Lined journal to list daily gratitudes. Fits 1000+ gratitudes!

CONVERSATIONS JOURNAL

Lined journal for writing out morning or evening prayers.

MEN'S PRAYER JOURNAL

6-month undated prayer journal with prompts and sections to fill out before the 1st, then pray throughout the month.

KID'S PRAYER JOURNAL

6-month undated prayer journal for kids ages 6-12 with sections to fill out and pray throughout the month.

PREGNANCY PRAYER JOURNAL

A prayer journal to pray throughout pregnancy and beyond including Scripture to encourage you during labor and delivery.

AVAILABLE AT VALMARIEPAPER.COM

Made in the USA
Lexington, KY
09 May 2018